特長と使い方

JN084439

～本書を活用した大学入試対策～

□ **志望校を決める（調べる・考える）**
　入試日程，受験科目，出題範囲，レベルなどが決まるので，やるべきことが見えやすくなります。

□ **「合格」までのスケジュールを決める**
　基礎固め・苦手克服期 … 受験勉強スタート～入試の6か月前頃
　・教科書レベルの問題を解けるようにします。
　・苦手分野をなくしましょう。
　⊖ 英文法の理解が不安な人は，
　　『**大学入試 ステップアップ 英文法【基礎】**』に取り組みましょう。

　応用力養成期 … 入試の6か月前～3か月前頃
　・身につけた基礎を土台にして，入試レベルの問題に対応できる応用力を養成します。
　・志望校の過去問を確認して，出題傾向，解答の形式などを把握しておきましょう。
　・模試を積極的に活用しましょう。模試で課題などが見つかったら，『**大学入試 ステップアップ 英文法【基礎】**』で復習して，確実に解けるようにしておきましょう。

　実戦力養成期 … 入試の3か月前頃～入試直前
　・時間配分や解答の形式を踏まえ，できるだけ本番に近い状態で過去問に取り組みましょう。

志望校合格！！

📖 英語の学習法

◎ **同じ問題を何度も繰り返し解く**
　多くの教材に取り組むよりも，1つの教材を何度も繰り返し解く方が力がつきます。
　⊖『**大学入試 ステップアップ 英文法【基礎】**』の活用例を，次のページで紹介しています。

◎ **解けない問題こそ実力アップのチャンス**
　間違えた問題の解説を読んでも理解できないときは，解説を1行ずつ丁寧に理解しながら読むまたは書き写して，自分のつまずき箇所を明確にしましょう。教科書レベルの内容がよく理解できないときは，さらに前に戻って復習することも大切です。

◎ **基本問題は確実に解けるようにする**
　応用問題も基本問題の組み合わせです。まずは基本問題が確実に解けるようにしましょう。解ける基本問題が増えていくことで，応用力も必ず身についてきます。

◎ **ケアレスミス対策**
　日頃から，問題をよく読んで答える習慣を身につけ，実際の試験でも解いた後に再度確認し，ケアレスミスを1つでもなくせるように注意しましょう。

～本書のしくみ～

本冊

🖐 **要点整理**
重要事項をまとめています。ひとつひとつ確実に理解し，覚えましょう。

見開き２ページで１単元完結。
簡潔かつ明快な英文で構成。

☆ **重要な問題**
ぜひ取り組んでおきたい問題です。状況に応じて効率よく学習を進めるときの目安にもなります。

check 1
重要事項の確認問題です。わからない場合は，もう一度，要点整理を確認しましょう。

advice
つまずきそうな問題には，適宜ヒントを掲載しています。

解答・解説

解答部分を赤く示し，解説との見分けをつきやすく工夫したので，答え合わせがしやすくなっています。

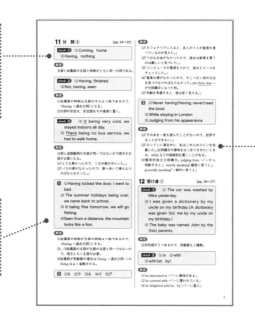

詳しい解説つきです。正誤確認だけでなく，解答するときのポイントになる文法解説も注目しましょう。

「解答→解説」の順に配列しているので，大問単位でしっかり理解を深められます。

📖 本書の活用例

◎ 何度も繰り返し取り組むとき，１巡目は全問→２巡目は１巡目に間違った問題→３巡目は２巡目に間違った問題 …のように進めて，全問解けるようになるまで繰り返します。

◎ ざっと全体を復習したいときは，各単元の要点整理だけ取り組むと効率的です。

目　次

Date

本書に関する最新情報は, 小社ホームページにある**本書の「サポート情報」**をご覧ください。(開設していない場合もございます。)
なお, この本の内容についての責任は小社にあり, 内容に関するご質問は直接小社におよせください。

3

01 | 基本文型

解答 ▶ 別冊p.1

🖑 要点整理

❶ 基本文型

(1) **第1文型**(S + V)……補語・目的語を必要としない**完全自動詞**の構文。

S(主語)	V(動詞)	M(修飾語句)
The shops	close	on Sundays.
Water	freezes	at 0° C.

(2) **第2文型**(S + V + C)……主格補語を必要とする**不完全自動詞**の構文。

S	V	C(補語)	M
The fat man	was	tired	after running.
She	looks	pretty	in white.

(3) **第3文型**(S + V + O)……目的語を1つとる**完全他動詞**の構文。

S	V	O(目的語)	M
We	grow	vegetables	in our garden.
My sister	enjoyed	traveling	by car.

(4) **第4文型**(S + V + IO + DO)……目的語を2つとる**授与動詞**の構文。

S	V	IO(人)	DO(物)
My uncle	gave	me	a nice present.
Nancy	bought	her daughter	a pretty dress.

(5) **第5文型**(S + V + O + C)……目的語と目的格補語をとる**不完全他動詞**の構文。

S	V	O	C
We	called	the old man	Big John.
I	found	this book	very interesting.

check 1 次の各文の下線部に S(主語),V(動詞),C(補語),O(目的語),M(修飾語句)の記号をつけよ。

(1) The guests praised the picture hanging on the wall.

(2) His bad behavior made his father angry.

(3) He is not what he was ten years ago.

(4) This pen writes very well.

(5) The machine will save you a great deal of trouble.

1 次の各文の下線部の語句が，目的語(O)か補語(C)かを答えよ。

(1) When I grow up, I will become a nurse. （　　　）

(2) Will you show me how to use this camera? （　　　）

(3) She sent us a postcard from England. （　　　）

(4) Our new teacher seems nice. （　　　）

2 次の各文の文型を指摘せよ。

(1) This shirt cost me 4,000 yen. 第（　）文型

(2) The theater you are looking for is in front of the bank. 第（　）文型

(3) Your desk feels strong. 第（　）文型

(4) I believe him to be innocent. 第（　）文型

(5) Our teacher suggested another plan to us. 第（　）文型

☆ **3** 次の各文を〈S ＋ V ＋ O ＋前置詞～〉の文型に書き換えよ。

(1) He showed us his album.

_____

(2) He bought his wife a fur coat.

_____

(3) The teacher told us a mysterious story yesterday.

_____

☆ **4** 次の各組の文を，動詞の意味の違いに注意して，日本語に直せ。

(1) ① She turned pale to hear the news.
　（　　　　　　　　　　　　　　　　　　　　　　）
② She turned to the left at the corner.
　（　　　　　　　　　　　　　　　　　　　　　　）

(2) ① My father runs every morning to stay healthy.
　（　　　　　　　　　　　　　　　　　　　　　　）
② My father runs a Chinese restaurant in the center of the city.
　（　　　　　　　　　　　　　　　　　　　　　　）

(3) ① He left his son a great fortune.
　（　　　　　　　　　　　　　　　　　　　　　　）
② He left his son alone.
　（　　　　　　　　　　　　　　　　　　　　　　）

(4) ① I found the English book easily.
　（　　　　　　　　　　　　　　　　　　　　　　）
② I found the English book easy.
　（　　　　　　　　　　　　　　　　　　　　　　）

advice

3 例 My uncle gave me a nice present. → My uncle gave a nice present to me.

要点整理

❶ **基本時制**

(1) **現在時制**……現在の状態・習慣などを表す。

> My mother **knows** you very well. 〔状態〕

> My father **goes** to work by subway. 〔習慣〕

> Honesty **is** the best policy. 〔真理〕

> Our train **leaves** at six o'clock. 〔発着の予定〕

> Please wait here *till* I **come** back. 〔副詞節内での未来形の代用〕

(2) **過去時制**……過去の状態・動作・習慣などを表す。

> I **was** on the basketball team last year. 〔状態〕

> My uncle **went** to church every Sunday. 〔習慣〕

> I thought he **was** angry. 〔時制の一致〕

(3) **未来時制**……未来における状態・動作などを表す。

> My son **will** be three years old next month. 〔単純未来〕

> I **will** try my best in everything. 〔主語の意志〕

check 1 次の各文の（　）内から適当なものを選べ。

(1) I will put off my departure if it (will rain, rains) tomorrow.

(2) I wonder if it (will rain, rains) tomorrow.

(3) She (went, goes) shopping on Sundays these days.

(4) He (studies, studied) English when he was in America.

(5) The plane that we are waiting for (arrive, arrives, arriving) soon.

(6) I thought he (has, had, will have) a cell phone, but he didn't.

(7) We learned that nothing (travels, traveled, to travel) faster than light.

❷ **未来を表す他の表現**

be going to ～「～するつもりだ」……近い未来などを表す場合に用いる。

be about to ～「まさに～しようとしている」

check 2 次の各文を日本語に直せ。

(1) I am going to spend my summer holidays in England.

（　　　　　　　　　　　　　　　　　　　　　　　　　　　　）

(2) Don't go out. We are about to have lunch.

（　　　　　　　　　　　　　　　　　　　　　　　　　　　　）

☆ **1** 次の各文の（　）内の動詞を適当な形にせよ。

(1) I wonder if he (succeed) in the exam next year.　　　　　　　＿＿＿＿＿＿＿＿

(2) I didn't know that gold (be) heavier than lead.　　　　　　　　＿＿＿＿＿＿＿＿

(3) You must not cross the road until the light (change) to green.　[愛知学院大]

　　　　　　　　　　　　　　　　　　　　　　　　　　　　　　＿＿＿＿＿＿＿＿

(4) I (buy) this car two years ago.　　　　　　　　　　　　　　＿＿＿＿＿＿＿＿

(5) My father never (smoke) when he is at table.　　　　　　　　＿＿＿＿＿＿＿＿

(6) I can't remember where I (see) him last.　　　　　　　　　　＿＿＿＿＿＿＿＿

☆ **2** 次の各文の（　）内から適当なものを選べ。

(1) It (is about to rain，rained，was raining). We should hurry.

(2) She said she (will，is，would) call me when she arrived.

(3) Hot air (go，gone，will go) up.

(4) My grandfather (takes，took，will take) a walk around the lake in those days.

(5) I will begin to make dinner when this TV program (is，was，will be) over.

3 次の各文が文法的に正しければＴを，誤っていればＦを（　）に書け。

(1) Let's go out of here before she will get angry.　　　　　　　　（　　）

(2) When I was five, my father told me that a year has 365 days.　　（　　）

(3) He is going to leave for Berlin yesterday.　　　　　　　　　　（　　）

(4) Bob and I enjoyed fishing in the river every summer.　　　　　（　　）

(5) Do you know when he will finish the job?　　　　　　　　　　（　　）

(6) When have they visited Kyoto?　　　　　　　　　　　　　　　（　　）

(7) Oil will float on water.　　　　　　　　　　　　　　　　　　（　　）

4 次の各組の英文がほぼ同じ内容になるように，＿＿に適当な語を入れよ。

(1) { When will you visit your uncle?
　　{ When ＿＿＿＿＿＿ you ＿＿＿＿＿＿ ＿＿＿＿＿＿ visit your uncle?

(2) { Paul said, "I'm feeling ill."
　　{ Paul said that ＿＿＿＿＿＿ ＿＿＿＿＿＿ feeling ill.

advice
....
3(6)疑問詞 when は，時の１点を明確に問う副詞であり，現在完了形の文には使えない。

7

03 | 完了形・進行形

月　　日

解答 ▶ 別冊pp.2-3

要点整理

❶ 完了形

(1) **現在完了**……過去の事柄との関係で，現在どうなっているかを表現する。

> Mary **has been** in hospital *since* the accident. 〔継続〕
> I **have been** to America only once. 〔経験〕
> Mother is not here; she **has gone** shopping. 〔結果〕

(2) **過去完了**……過去のある時を基準にして，その時までの継続・経験・完了と結果を表現する。

> He *died* after he **had been** ill for a long time. 〔継続〕
> *Until yesterday*, I **had** never **heard** of it. 〔経験〕
> My parents **had** already **eaten** dinner *by the time I got home*. 〔完了〕

(3) **未来完了**……未来のある時を基準にして，その時までの継続・経験・完了と結果を表現する。

> We**'ll have been** here for a year *next Friday*. 〔継続〕
> I **will have been** to Hawaii three times *if* I *go there again*. 〔経験〕
> I **will have finished** my homework *by ten o'clock*. 〔完了〕

check 1 次の各文の（　）内の動詞を指定された形にせよ。

(1) I (lose) my umbrella. 〔現在完了形に〕　　　　　＿＿＿＿＿＿＿

(2) We (live) in Fukuoka before we moved. 〔過去完了形に〕　　　＿＿＿＿＿＿＿

(3) He didn't know that I (buy) the watch. 〔過去完了形に〕　　　＿＿＿＿＿＿＿

(4) I (finish) my homework in an hour. 〔未来完了形に〕　　　＿＿＿＿＿＿＿

❷ 進行形

> Don't take the newspaper away. **I'm** still **reading** it. 〔現在進行形〕
> I burnt my hand while I **was cooking**. 〔過去進行形〕
> The baby **has been crying** for almost ten minutes. 〔現在完了進行形〕
> Her eyes were red because she **had been crying**. 〔過去完了進行形〕
> I**'ll have been teaching** for ten years this summer. 〔未来完了進行形〕

check 2 次の各文の（　）内の動詞を指示された形にせよ。

(1) He (write) a letter in the room. 〔現在完了進行形に〕　　　＿＿＿＿＿＿＿

(2) Someone (knock) at the door. 〔過去進行形に〕　　　＿＿＿＿＿＿＿

(3) It (rain) at this time tomorrow. 〔未来進行形に〕　　　＿＿＿＿＿＿＿

☆ **1** 次の各文を日本語に直せ。

(1) Have you read the book you borrowed at the library yet?

(　　　　　　　　　　　　　　　　　　　　　　　　　　　　　　　)

(2) He hadn't met me for a long time until last year.

(　　　　　　　　　　　　　　　　　　　　　　　　　　　　　　　)

(3) Had you visited Los Angeles before we went there together?

(　　　　　　　　　　　　　　　　　　　　　　　　　　　　　　　)

(4) We will have been married for thirty years next month.

(　　　　　　　　　　　　　　　　　　　　　　　　　　　　　　　)

(5) He has been playing a video game since he got up.

(　　　　　　　　　　　　　　　　　　　　　　　　　　　　　　　)

(6) I will be crying at the stadium at this time of tomorrow.

(　　　　　　　　　　　　　　　　　　　　　　　　　　　　　　　)

2 次の各文の( )内に下から適当なものを選び，記号で答えよ。

(1) When I was in junior high school, I (　　　　) to the basketball club. 　　　[東京国際大]

　　ア belonged 　 イ belong 　 ウ was belonging 　 エ was belonged

(2) I heard that Mr. Suzuki (　　　　) jobs five times before coming to this office. 　[名城大]

　　ア changes 　 イ has changed 　 ウ was changed 　 エ had changed

(3) I (　　　　) piano lessons since 1998. 　　　　[大阪商業大]

　　ア took 　 イ am taking 　 ウ was taking 　 エ have been taking

(4) Ellen will be able to go to the party if she (　　　　) her work.

　　ア has done 　 イ will do 　 ウ will have done 　 エ had done

3 日本語を参考に，＿＿に適当な語を入れよ。

(1) 彼女はその老人には以前，何度か会ったと言った。 　　　　[成蹊大-改]

　　She said that she ＿＿＿＿＿ ＿＿＿＿＿ the old man several times ＿＿＿＿＿.

(2) 母はちょうど駅に父を見送りに行ってきたところだ。

　　My mother ＿＿＿＿＿ just ＿＿＿＿＿ ＿＿＿＿＿ the station to see my father off.

(3) 私が宿題を済ませてしまうまで，少し待ってください。

　　Please wait for a while until I ＿＿＿＿＿ ＿＿＿＿＿ my homework.

(4) あなたは彼の親切を疑ってばかりいる。

　　＿＿＿＿＿ always ＿＿＿＿＿ his kindness.

advice ···
　2(4), **3**(3)意味の上では未来完了であるが，時を表す副詞節の中では？

9

🖰 要点整理

❶ 助動詞 will / shall / can

(1) **will と would**

> I **will** be twenty-five next week. 〔単純未来〕
> My brother **won't** let me drive his car. 〔現在の意志〕
> Grandfather **will** sit reading all day long. 〔現在の習慣・習性〕
> He **would not** tell us where the money was hidden. 〔過去の意志〕
> We **would** often go fishing on Sundays. 〔過去の習慣・習性〕
> **Would** you please give me another cup of tea? 〔丁寧な依頼〕

(2) **shall と should**

> **Shall I** carry your bag upstairs? 〔相手の意向を尋ねる〕
> Where **shall** we go this evening? 〔提案〕
> You **should** be kind to others. 〔義務・当然〕
> If you leave now, you **should** arrive there by six. 〔当然の推量〕
> They suggested that I **should** accept his kind offer.
> 〔要求・必要・提案を表す that 節内で用いる〕
> It is surprising that he **should** be so rude to you.
> 〔驚き・怒りなどの感情の原因を表す that 節内で用いる〕

(3) **can と could，be able to 〜**

> He **can** speak English fluently. 〔能力〕
>   = He is able to speak English fluently.
> You will **be able to** walk again in a few weeks. 〔助動詞＋ be able to 〜〕
> That **can't** be the postman— it's only seven o'clock. 〔否定的推量〕
> You **can** borrow the book, but return it tomorrow. 〔許可〕
> **Could** I see your passport, please? 〔丁寧な依頼〕

check 1 次の各文の（　）内から適当なものを選べ。

(1) (Would，Should) you like another cup of tea?

(2) I (will，would) often visit the museum when I was young.

(3) You (shall，should) not break your promise.

(4) He (can，can't) be ill. I met him yesterday.

(5) This box (won't，can't) shut; there are too many things in it.

(6) It is necessary that you (will，should) study abroad.

1 日本語を参考に，＿＿＿に適当な語を入れよ。

(1) 彼は東京に来ると，よくその美術館を訪れたものだ。

When he came up to Tokyo, he ＿＿＿＿＿＿ often visit the museum.

(2) 彼がそんなことをするとは不思議だ。 [愛媛大-改]

It is strange that he ＿＿＿＿＿＿ do such a thing.

(3) あんなにたくさん食べたのだから，空腹のはずがない。

After eating such a big meal, you ＿＿＿＿＿＿ be hungry.

(4) 私は最近よく眠れないのです。

I haven't ＿＿＿＿＿＿ able to sleep well recently.

(5) 私は彼女に忠告しようとするのだが，どうしても聞こうとしない。

I've tried to give her advice, but she ＿＿＿＿＿＿ listen.

☆ **2** 次の各組の英文がほぼ同じ内容になるように，＿＿＿に適当な語を入れよ。

(1) { They were able to find the post office soon.
{ They ＿＿＿＿＿＿ find the post office soon.

(2) { Do you want me to bring you a newspaper?
{ ＿＿＿＿＿＿ I bring you a newspaper?

(3) { Let's have a break.
{ ＿＿＿＿＿＿ we have a break?

(4) { I know how to use this machine.
{ I ＿＿＿＿＿＿ use this machine.

(5) { The doctor advised me to take a walk every morning.
{ The doctor advised that I ＿＿＿＿＿＿ take a walk every morning.

3 次の各組の文を，下線部の意味の違いに注意して，日本語に直せ。

(1) { ① Takashi lived in Singapore, so he <u>can</u> speak English and Chinese.
{ 　（　　　　　　　　　　　　　　　　　　　　　　　　　　　　　）
{ ② Takashi is now in Singapore, so he <u>can't</u> be here.
{ 　（　　　　　　　　　　　　　　　　　　　　　　　　　　　　　）

(2) { ① We <u>should</u> take a bus. We don't have much time.
{ 　（　　　　　　　　　　　　　　　　　　　　　　　　　　　　　）
{ ② If you take a bus, it <u>should</u> take about an hour.
{ 　（　　　　　　　　　　　　　　　　　　　　　　　　　　　　　）

(3) { ① I <u>would</u> like to have some water.
{ 　（　　　　　　　　　　　　　　　　　　　　　　　　　　　　　）
{ ② The boy <u>wouldn't</u> drink the milk because it smelled bad.
{ 　（　　　　　　　　　　　　　　　　　　　　　　　　　　　　　）

advice
1 (2)感情の原因を表す that 節の中で用いる助動詞は？

05 | 助動詞 ②

📌 要点整理

❶ **助動詞 may / must / need / dare**

(1) **may と might**

> **May** I turn on the TV?〔許可〕

> You **may** feel better tomorrow.〔推量〕

> **May** God bless you!〔祈願〕

> **Might** I borrow your pen for a minute?〔丁寧な依頼〕

(2) **must**

> You **must** wait till the light turns to green.〔命令〕

> I **must** look funny with this hat on.〔may より強い推量〕

(3) **need と dare**……本動詞としても用いられる。

> You **needn't** *go*.〔助動詞〕

> He **dare not** *speak* to her.〔助動詞〕

> You **don't need to** go.〔本動詞〕

> He **doesn't dare to** speak to her.〔本動詞〕

check 1 次の各文の（　）内から適当なものを選べ。

(1) (May，Must) I leave now?— No, you must not.

(2) He (must，need) have a fever; his face is red.

(3) You (need，dare) not come if you don't want to.

❷ **助動詞 ought to / used to**

> You **ought to** (= should) look after your dog better.〔義務・当然・必要〕

> It **ought to** be windy today.〔当然の推量・可能性の高い推量〕

> We **used to** go to that restaurant a lot.〔過去の習慣〕

check 2 次の各文の（　）内から適当なものを選べ。

(1) His hair (used，ought) to be black; it's white now.

(2) He looks feverish, so he (used，ought) to see a doctor.

❸ **助動詞＋ have ＋過去分詞** 発展

(1)～(3)過去に対する推量や，(4)過去において実行されなかった行為を批判的に述べる場合などに用いられる。

(1) Why isn't he here? He **must have missed** the train.

(2) Kate didn't answer the phone. She **may have been** asleep.

(3) John **can't have read** this book. It's too difficult.

(4) You **should have knocked** before you came in.

☆ **1** 次の各文を日本語に直せ。

(1) You must not smoke at this restaurant.

(   )

(2) It must be difficult to finish reading this book in a week.

(   )

(3) How dare you come so late at night?

(   )

(4) You ought not to stay in your room on such a sunny day.

(   )

(5) I used to play volleyball with the members of the club.

(   )

2 次の各組の英文がほぼ同じ内容になるように，＿＿に適当な語を入れよ。

(1) { I hope you'll do well in the exam.
     { ＿＿＿＿＿ you do well in the exam!

(2) { I think we should return to the hotel soon.   ［南山大—改］
     { I think we ＿＿＿＿＿ to return to the hotel soon.

(3) { You don't have to start at once.
     { You ＿＿＿＿＿ start at once.

(4) { Judy must be careless because she did such a thing.
     { Judy ＿＿＿＿＿ be careful because she did such a thing.

3 日本語を参考に，＿＿に適当な語を入れよ。

(1) 彼女は今ごろはもう事務所に到着しているはずだ。

She ＿＿＿＿＿ to ＿＿＿＿＿ ＿＿＿＿＿ at her office by now.

(2) 僕を起こさなくてもよかったのに。仕事に行かなくてもいいんだ。

You ＿＿＿＿＿ ＿＿＿＿＿ ＿＿＿＿＿ me up; I don't have to go to work.

(3) 彼の車がここにないから，きっと行ってしまったに違いない。

His car isn't here, so he ＿＿＿＿＿ ＿＿＿＿＿ ＿＿＿＿＿ .

(4) ジョンはまだここに来ていない。彼はバスに乗り遅れたのかもしれない。

John hasn't come yet. He ＿＿＿＿＿ ＿＿＿＿＿ ＿＿＿＿＿ the bus.

(5) ジェーンがこの数学の宿題を1人でやったはずがない。

Jane ＿＿＿＿＿ ＿＿＿＿＿ ＿＿＿＿＿ this math homework for herself.

advice ....
2(1)「あなたが試験でうまくやれますように。」祈願文。

06 | 不定詞 ①

🖐 要点整理

❶ 不定詞の基本用法

不定詞には，**名詞的用法**（主語・補語・目的語となる），**形容詞的用法**（名詞・代名詞を修飾），**副詞的用法**（動詞・形容詞・副詞を修飾）がある。

check 1 次の不定詞の用法を述べよ。

(1) The only thing we can do is to call the police.　　　　　　（　　　　　）

(2) I'm pleased to hear about your marriage.　　　　　　（　　　　　）

(3) Is there anything to eat for lunch?　　　　　　（　　　　　）

❷ 不定詞の意味上の主語

不定詞の主語は，文の主語と一致する場合や，不特定の人の場合は特に示されない。**意味上の主語**を示したいときは，〈**for ＋人＋ to ～**〉または〈**of ＋人＋ to ～**〉の形で示す。また，動詞の目的語が不定詞の意味上の主語となることもある（〈want〔ask〕＋人＋ to ～〉など）。

check 2 次の各文の適当な位置に，（　）内の語を入れよ。必要ならば適当な語をつけ加えること。

(1) The doctor advised to give up drinking. (me)

_____

(2) It is impossible to read a hundred pages in an hour. (you)

_____

(3) It is very careless to do such a thing! (him)

_____

❸ 完了不定詞

不定詞の時制が，述語動詞より前の「時」を表す場合は，〈**to have ＋過去分詞**〉の形を用いる。

check 3 次の各組の英文がほぼ同じ内容になるように，____ に適当な語を入れよ。

(1) { It seems that she was an actress when she was young.
　　 She seems _____ _____ _____ an actress when she was young.

(2) { It seemed that he had been ill for a long time.
　　 He seemed _____ _____ _____ ill for a long time.

(3) { It is reported that many people were injured in the accident.
　　 Many people are _____ _____ _____ been injured in the accident.

1 次の各文の＿＿に適当な語を入れよ。

(1) ＿＿＿＿＿＿ is dangerous to swim in this river.

(2) It is silly ＿＿＿＿＿＿ you to trust him.

(3) She is believed ＿＿＿＿＿＿ be over ninety.

(4) My mother taught me ＿＿＿＿＿＿ to play the violin.

(5) It is good ＿＿＿＿＿＿ us to take exercise every morning.

☆ **2** 次の各組の英文がほぼ同じ内容になるように，与えられた語句に続けて不定詞を用いて書き換えよ。

(1) ⎰ We have no house that we can live in.
   ⎱ We have no house ＿＿＿＿＿＿＿＿＿＿＿＿＿＿＿＿＿＿＿＿＿＿＿＿＿.

(2) ⎰ She didn't know what she should do next.
   ⎱ She didn't know ＿＿＿＿＿＿＿＿＿＿＿＿＿＿＿＿＿＿＿＿＿＿＿.

(3) ⎰ To obey the law is everybody's duty.
   ⎱ It is ＿＿＿＿＿＿＿＿＿＿＿＿＿＿＿＿＿＿＿＿＿＿＿＿＿＿＿＿.

(4) ⎰ You are very kind to help me.
   ⎱ It is ＿＿＿＿＿＿＿＿＿＿＿＿＿＿＿＿＿＿＿＿＿＿＿＿＿＿＿.

(5) ⎰ It seems that they got lost in the fog.
   ⎱ They seem ＿＿＿＿＿＿＿＿＿＿＿＿＿＿＿＿＿＿＿＿＿＿＿＿＿＿.

3 日本語を参考に，（ ）内の語句を並べかえよ。

(1) お待たせしてすみません。

Sorry (to / you / waiting / kept / have). ［九州産業大］

Sorry ＿＿＿＿＿＿＿＿＿＿＿＿＿＿＿＿＿＿＿＿＿＿＿＿＿＿＿＿.

(2) 風が強かったので，彼女は孫たちに外出しないよう言った。

She (her / not / told / to / go / grandchildren / out) because it was windy.

She ＿＿＿＿＿＿＿＿＿＿＿＿＿＿＿＿＿＿＿＿＿ because it was windy.

(3) 濃いお茶をお入れしましょうか。 ［東京家政大］

Would (make / me / to / like / for / you / tea / strong) you?

Would ＿＿＿＿＿＿＿＿＿＿＿＿＿＿＿＿＿＿＿＿＿＿＿＿ you?

(4) あなたは私の忠告を聞きさえすればよいのです。

All (is / follow / have / you / do / to) my advice.

All ＿＿＿＿＿＿＿＿＿＿＿＿＿＿＿＿＿＿＿＿＿＿＿＿ my advice.

advice ┄┄┄
1 (2) silly「まぬけな」 人の性質を表す形容詞。
2 (5) 完了不定詞を用いる。

15

07 | 不定詞 ②

🖐 要点整理

❶ 原形不定詞

　　感覚動詞(hear, see, feel など)，使役動詞(make, have, let など)の目的格補語，**had better 〜**「〜したほうがよい」，**cannot (help) but 〜**「〜 せざるを得ない」の後ろなどでは**原形不定詞**を用いる。ただし，使役動詞として使われる get のみ，〈**get ＋人＋ to 〜**〉を用いる。

check 1 次の各文の(　)内から適当なものを選べ。

(1) Have you ever heard him (speak，to speak) ill of others?

(2) You had better (not follow，not to follow) his advice.

(3) We couldn't but (cry，crying) for help.

(4) Our boss made us (work，to work) till late.

(5) We couldn't get her (accept，to accept) the offer.

❷ 不定詞の慣用表現

　　cannot afford to 〜「〜 する余裕がない」，**manage to 〜**「何とか〜する」，**never fail to 〜**「必ず〜する」，**... enough to 〜**「〜するのに十分…だ」，**too ... to 〜**「〜するには…すぎる」，**so ... as to 〜**「〜するほどに…だ」，**in order to 〜＝ so as to 〜**「〜するために」などがある。

check 2 次の各組の英文がほぼ同じ内容になるように，＿＿に適当な語を入れよ。

(1) ⎰ The woman spoke so fast that I couldn't understand her.
　　⎱ The woman spoke ＿＿＿＿＿ fast for me ＿＿＿＿＿ understand.

(2) ⎰ I got up early so as to be in time for school.
　　⎱ I got up early in ＿＿＿＿＿ ＿＿＿＿＿ be in time for school.

(3) ⎰ She was kind enough to show me the way.
　　⎱ She was ＿＿＿＿＿ kind ＿＿＿＿＿ to show me the way.

❸ 独立不定詞 発展

　　文の時制などの要素とは関係なく用いられ，**to tell the truth**「実を言うと」，**needless to say**「言うまでもなく」，**to say nothing of 〜**「〜 は言うまでもなく」，**strange to say**「奇妙なことに」，**to begin with**「まず第一に」，**to be sure**「確かに」，**so to speak**「いわば」，**to make matters worse**「さらに悪いことに」などの慣用表現がある。

> **To do him justice**, he is an experienced doctor.
　　「公平に評価すれば」

> He can speak German, **not to mention** English.
　　　　「英語は言うまでもなく」

★ **1** 次の各組の英文がほぼ同じ内容になるように，＿＿＿に適当な語を入れよ。

(1)
- This problem is beyond me.
- This problem is _____ difficult _____ me to solve.

(2)
- It was very kind of him to help me with my homework.
- He was kind _____ _____ help me with my homework.

(3)
- We worked hard in order that we could go to college.
- We worked hard _____ _____ to go to college.

(4)
- She was nice enough to lend me some money.
- She was _____ nice _____ to lend me some money.

(5)
- As I don't have enough money, I cannot buy that car.
- I cannot _____ _____ buy that car.

(6)
- It would be better for you to go to the dentist at once.
- You had _____ _____ to the dentist at once.

(7)
- He always takes a walk before breakfast every morning.
- He never _____ _____ take a walk before breakfast every morning.

2 次の各文の（　）内から適当なものを選べ。

(1) I saw him (cross，to cross，to be crossing) the street.

(2) The floor was felt (shake，to shake，shaken).

(3) I'll have my son (washed，wash，to wash，have washed) the car tomorrow.　　[東京国際大]

(4) You had (not better，better not，better not to) sit up late at night.

(5) I'll have to get Jack (fix，to fix，to fixed，fixed) the car.　　[四天王寺大]

3 次の各文の（　）内に下から適当なものを選び，記号で答えよ。

(1) To（　　　　　）matters worse, it began to snow.

(2) To（　　　　　）with, let's go camping near the lake.

(3) To（　　　　　）the truth, I cannot rely on you.

(4) To（　　　　　）sure, it's a very good idea.

(5) He is poor at Chinese, to（　　　　　）nothing of English.

(6) He is, so to（　　　　　）, a walking dictionary.

　〔**ア** say　**イ** be　**ウ** tell　**エ** make　**オ** speak　**カ** begin〕

advice ···
1 (2)〈形容詞 + enough to ～〉の構文。
　　(5)「私はその車を買う余裕がない。」の意味。

08 | 動名詞 ①

🖐 要点整理

❶ 動名詞と現在分詞

　　動名詞は名詞の性格を持ち，**主語・目的語などの働き**をする。また，名詞の用途を示す修飾語としても用いられる。形の上では現在分詞（～している）と同じ。

check 1 下線部の各語が，①動名詞か，②現在分詞かを番号で答えよ。

(1) Taking a walk is good for our health. 　　　　　　　　　　（　　　　　）

(2) Be careful in crossing the busy street. 　　　　　　　　　（　　　　　）

(3) My grandfather is taking a walk in the park now. 　　　　（　　　　　）

(4) Look at the baby sleeping in the bed. 　　　　　　　　　　（　　　　　）

(5) You are allowed to smoke only in the smoking room. 　　　（　　　　　）

❷ 動名詞の意味上の主語

　　文の主語と異なる場合には，名詞・代名詞の**所有格**または**目的格**をその**前**に置く。

check 2 次の各組の文を，意味の違いに注意して，日本語に直せ。

(1)
① He is proud of being a famous doctor.
　（　　　　　　　　　　　　　　　　　　　　　　　　　　　）
② He is proud of his father ('s) being a famous doctor.
　（　　　　　　　　　　　　　　　　　　　　　　　　　　　）

(2)
① I am sure of succeeding in the exam.
　（　　　　　　　　　　　　　　　　　　　　　　　　　　　）
② I am sure of his succeeding in the exam.
　（　　　　　　　　　　　　　　　　　　　　　　　　　　　）

❸ 動名詞の注意すべき用法

　　否定形は不定詞・分詞と同様に，**否定語**をその**前**に置く。また，述語動詞より前の「時」を，〈**having ＋過去分詞**〉の形で表す。

check 3 次の各組の英文がほぼ同じ内容になるように，＿＿に適当な語を入れよ。

(1)
I am sorry that I broke my promise.
I am sorry for ＿＿＿＿＿ ＿＿＿＿＿ my promise.

(2)
I regret that I didn't work hard when young.
I regret ＿＿＿＿＿ ＿＿＿＿＿ worked hard when young.

1 次の各文の（　）内に下から適当なものを選び，記号で答えよ。

(1) (　　　　　) papers rapidly is not as important as writing them well.　　　　　［亜細亜大］

　ア Written　　イ Writing　　ウ Write　　エ Wrote

(2) We can preserve our environment (　　　　　).　　　　　［京都産業大-改］

　ア by recycling　　イ for do recycle　　ウ in means of recycle

　エ with doing recycle

(3) I am sorry for (　　　　　) you the truth.　　　　　［大阪経済大］

　ア don't tell　　イ haven't tell　　ウ not telling　　エ didn't telling

(4) I don't like (　　　　　) the car to him.　　　　　［東京国際大］

　ア for you to lend　　イ of you to lend　　ウ your lending　　エ so you lend

(5) Would you mind (　　　　　) here? —— Of course not.

　ア my sitting　　イ your sitting　　ウ to sit　　エ to be sitting

☆ **2** 次の各組の英文がほぼ同じ内容になるように，＿＿に適当な語を入れよ。

(1) { It is a lot of fun to swim on a hot day.
　　{ ＿＿＿＿＿＿ on a hot day is a lot of fun.

(2) { He denied that he had stolen the money.
　　{ He denied ＿＿＿＿＿＿ ＿＿＿＿＿＿ the money.

(3) { He insisted that I should respect my parents.
　　{ He insisted ＿＿＿＿＿＿ ＿＿＿＿＿＿ ＿＿＿＿＿＿ my parents.

(4) { She went out of the restaurant, but she didn't pay.
　　{ She went out of the restaurant ＿＿＿＿＿＿ paying.

(5) { Is there any hope that he will become president?
　　{ Is there any hope ＿＿＿＿＿＿ ＿＿＿＿＿＿ ＿＿＿＿＿＿ president?

3 日本語を参考に，＿＿に適当な語を入れよ。

(1) 英語を話すときは間違えるのを恐れてはいけません。　　　　　［崇城大-改］

　Don't be afraid ＿＿＿＿＿＿ ＿＿＿＿＿＿ mistakes in ＿＿＿＿＿＿ English.

(2) 彼は不当に扱われたと文句を言った。　　　　　［玉川大］

　He complained ＿＿＿＿＿＿ ＿＿＿＿＿＿ ＿＿＿＿＿＿ treated unfairly.

(3) 弟は宿題をしなかったのでしかられた。

　My brother was scolded for ＿＿＿＿＿＿ ＿＿＿＿＿＿ done his homework.

advice
2 (3) insist on 〜ing「〜することを主張する」
3 (3)動名詞を否定する。

要点整理

❶ 動名詞と不定詞

動詞によっては，**動名詞または不定詞のみ**を**目的語**にとるものがある。

動名詞…… avoid，deny，enjoy，give up，finish，mind，practice など。

不定詞…… choose，decide，expect，hope，learn，wish，promise など。

check 1 次の各文の（　）内から適当なものを選べ。

(1) Would you mind (to open，opening) the window?

(2) She stopped (to watch，watching) TV and went to bed.

(3) I like to practice (to play，playing) the flute.

(4) All of us enjoyed (to watch，watching) an exciting football game.

❷ 動名詞の注意すべき用法

目的語として，**動名詞と不定詞の両方**をとることはできるが，**意味の異なる**動詞がある。

remember，forget，try など。

check 2 次の各組の英文を，意味の違いに注意して，日本語に直せ。

① I remember reading this book once.

（　　　　　　　　　　　　　　　　　　　　　　　　　　　　）

② Please remember to read this book.

（　　　　　　　　　　　　　　　　　　　　　　　　　　　　）

❸ 動名詞の慣用表現

feel like ～ing「～したい気がする」，**There is no ～ing.**「～するのは不可能だ。」，**look forward to ～ing**「～することを楽しみにしている」，**be used to ～ing**「～するのに慣れている」，**on ～ing**「～するとすぐに」，**be worth ～ing**「～する価値がある」，**prevent〔keep〕＋ O ＋ from ～ing**「O が～するのを妨げる」などがある。

check 3 次の各組の英文がほぼ同じ内容になるように，＿＿に適当な語を入れよ。

(1) {
As soon as I arrived at the station, I went to see him.
＿＿＿＿＿ ＿＿＿＿＿ at the station, I went to see him.
}

(2) {
It is impossible to account for tastes.
There is ＿＿＿＿＿ ＿＿＿＿＿ for tastes.
}

(3) {
They couldn't go swimming because of the storm.
The storm ＿＿＿＿＿ them ＿＿＿＿＿ going swimming.
}

1 次の各文の（　）内から適当なものを選べ。

(1) You should avoid (to keep，keeping) company with them.

(2) I am looking forward to (see，seeing) you again.

(3) You will get used to (keep，keeping) early hours.

(4) We cannot help (to laugh，laughing) at his stupid idea.

(5) Don't forget (to mail，mailing) this letter tomorrow.

☆ **2** 次の各文の（　）内に下から適当なものを選び，記号で答えよ。

(1) Would you mind (　　　　　) this letter?　　　　　　　　　　　　　[中京大]

　　ア translate　　イ to translate　　ウ translating　　エ translated

(2) We decided (　　　　　) this project.　　　　　　　　　　　　　　[大阪商業大]

　　ア continue　　イ to continue　　ウ continued　　エ continuing

(3) It (　　　　　) without saying that Japanese is a difficult language to learn.

　　ア has　　イ takes　　ウ goes　　エ passes

(4) He tried (　　　　　) the piano, but he couldn't.　　　　　　　　　[立命館大]

　　ア having played　　イ playing of　　ウ to have played　　エ to play

(5) He had to give up (　　　　　) because of the health problems.

　　ア smoke　　イ to smoke　　ウ smoking　　エ smoked

(6) There is (　　　　　) which team will win the game.　　　　　　　[東京理科大]

　　ア no telling　　イ not telling in　　ウ not to tell　　エ not having told

(7) I remember (　　　　　) with my brother in the park when we were children.　[日本女子大]

　　ア played　　イ playing　　ウ to have played　　エ to play

3 次の各文の＿＿＿にＡ，......にＢから適当な語を選び，Ｂは正しい形にして入れよ。

(1) My sister is good ＿＿＿＿＿ .... pictures.

(2) Bad weather kept me ＿＿＿＿＿ .... the party.

(3) Kyoto is ＿＿＿＿＿ .... again.

(4) I'm not used ＿＿＿＿＿ .... so much at lunchtime.　　　　　　　[東京家政大-改]

(5) I don't feel ＿＿＿＿＿ .... TV.

(6) I never see this picture ＿＿＿＿＿ .... of my grandmother.

　　A 〔to，from，like，worth，without，at〕

　　B 〔eat，think，attend，visit，paint，watch〕

advice
3(4)「私は昼食にそんなに多く食べることに慣れていない。」の意味。

10 | 分 詞 ①

要点整理

❶ 分詞の形容詞的用法

分詞には，**現在分詞**「～している」，**過去分詞**「～される」の２種類あり，**名詞の前後**に置かれて名詞を修飾する。また，**主格補語**，**目的格補語**に用いられる。

check 1 次の各文の（　）内の動詞を最も適当な形にせよ。

(1) (Bark) dogs don't always bite. _____

(2) The man (injure) in the accident was taken to the hospital. _____

(3) The boy (sit) on the sofa is my nephew. _____

(4) Grandmother sat (nod) by the fire. _____

(5) He found his name (write) on the list. _____

(6) I can make myself (understand) in English. _____

❷ have(get)＋O＋過去分詞

他人に「**～してもらう**」，「**～される**」の意味を表すには，この形を用いる。

check 2 日本語を参考に，（　）内の語句を並べかえよ。ただし，１語だけ適当な形に変化させること。

(1) 私は自転車を修理してもらった。I (my / repair / had / bicycle).
I _____.

(2) 私はカバンを盗まれた。I (bag / my / had / steal).
I _____.

---

1 次の各文の適当な位置に，（　）内の語句を入れよ。

(1) People like to visit the country. (living in the city)

_____

(2) He bought a book yesterday. (written in English)

_____

(3) My brother left the water. (running)

_____

(4) The people were all taken to the nearest hospital. (injured)

_____

(5) The number of people has not been known. (injured in the traffic accident)

_____

☆ **2** 次の各文の（　）内の語を最も適当な形にせよ。

(1) The carpenter repaired the (break) chair.　　　　［清泉女子大］　_____

(2) Her idea seemed very (interest) to me.　　　　　　　　　　　_____

(3) We need more food for an (increase) population.　　　　　　_____

(4) The ground was covered with (fall) leaves.　　　　　　　　_____

(5) It was very (surprise) news to me.　　　　　　　　　　　　_____

(6) When you hear your name (call), please enter this room.　　［大阪経済大］　_____

(7) He found an old man (lie) on the floor.　　　　　　　　　　_____

(8) My mother looked (surprise) at the news.　　　　　　　　　_____

3 次の各組の英文がほぼ同じ内容になるように，＿＿に適当な語を入れよ。

(1) { I will buy a computer someone owned before.
　　{ I will buy a _____ computer. (u で始まる語)

(2) { This apartment is empty.
　　{ There is nobody _____ in this apartment.

(3) { My father had me paint the wall.
　　{ My father had the wall _____ _____ me.

(4) { I think you have been waiting for me.　I'm sorry.
　　{ I'm sorry to _____ kept you _____.

(5) { Jane closed her eyes while she was listening to the story.
　　{ Jane was listening to the story with her eyes _____.

4 次の各文の＿＿に下から適当なものを選び，必要ならば正しい形に変えて入れよ。

(1) A little dog came _____ after me.

(2) I couldn't make myself _____ in the noisy room.

(3) A _____ man will catch at a straw.

(4) Mary had her passport _____ at the immigration office.　　　　［東京国際大］

(5) I want my hair _____ because it's too long.

〔stamp, drown, hear, run, cut〕

advice --

2 (2) interested「興味がわいた」，interesting「興味をわかせるような」
　　(5)・(8) surprised「驚いた」，surprising「驚くべき」
4 (2)原形不定詞 hear は誤り。

11 分 詞②

☞ 要点整理

❶ 分詞構文

　分詞構文の作り方は，①接続詞を省く，②副詞節の主語が主節の主語と同じなら省く，③動詞を**分詞**に変える。

check 1 次の各組の英文がほぼ同じ内容になるように，＿＿＿に適当な語を入れよ。

(1) $\begin{cases} \text{When I came home, I found the door unlocked.} \\ \text{_____ _____ , I found the door unlocked.} \end{cases}$

(2) $\begin{cases} \text{As I had nothing to do, I went to bed early.} \\ \text{_____ _____ to do, I went to bed early.} \end{cases}$

❷ 注意すべき分詞構文

　述語動詞より前の「時」を表すには，〈**having ＋過去分詞**〉の形を用いる。また，分詞を否定するには，**否定語を分詞の直前**に置く。

check 2 次の各組の英文がほぼ同じ内容になるように，＿＿＿に適当な語を入れよ。

(1) $\begin{cases} \text{As he had finished the work, he went for a walk.} \\ \text{_____ _____ the work, he went for a walk.} \end{cases}$

(2) $\begin{cases} \text{As I have not seen my son for a long time, I may not recognize him.} \\ \text{_____ _____ _____ my son for a long time, I may not recognize him.} \end{cases}$

❸ 独立分詞構文

　分詞と述語動詞がそれぞれの別の主語を持つ構文を**独立分詞構文**という。

check 3 次の各文を文法的に正しい英文にせよ。

(1) Being very cold, we stayed indoors all day.

＿＿＿＿＿＿＿＿＿＿＿＿＿＿＿＿＿＿＿＿＿＿＿＿＿＿＿＿

(2) Being no bus service, we had to walk home.

＿＿＿＿＿＿＿＿＿＿＿＿＿＿＿＿＿＿＿＿＿＿＿＿＿＿＿＿

❹ 慣用的独立分詞構文

　主語を常に明示しない慣用的な分詞構文がある。

generally speaking「一般的に言って」，**roughly speaking**「おおざっぱに言って」，**strictly speaking**「厳密に言って」，**judging from ～**「～ から判断すると」，**considering ～＝ taking ～ into consideration**「～ を考慮すると」

1 次の各文を分詞構文を用いて書き換えよ。

(1) After I had locked the door, I went to bed.

_____

(2) As the summer holidays were over, we came back to school.

_____

(3) If it is fine tomorrow, we will go fishing.

_____

(4) If the mountain is seen from a distance, it looks like a lion.

_____

☆ **2** 次の各文の(　)内に下から適当なものを選び，記号で答えよ。

(1) (　　　　　) the cafeteria, I saw a friend of mine eating lunch.　　　　　［大阪商業大-改］

　ア Enter　　イ Enters　　ウ Entered　　エ Entering

(2) (　　　　　) enough money, she found it difficult to buy a new car.　　　［日本大-改］

　ア Having　　イ Having paid　　ウ Not having　　エ Not having paid

(3) (　　　　　) on his computer, he checked his e-mail.　　　　　　　　　　［拓殖大］

　ア Turn　　イ Turns　　ウ Turned　　エ Having turned

(4) (　　　　　) no train service, we had to find another way to get there.

　ア Being　　イ There being　　ウ Been　　エ There been

(5) (　　　　　) his age, he looks young.　　　　　　　　　　　　　　　　　［大谷大］

　ア Considering　　イ Looking　　ウ Remembering　　エ Thinking

3 次の各文の(　)内の語句を並べかえよ。

(1) (having / read / never / the book), I cannot criticize it.

_____ , I cannot criticize it.

(2) (staying / London / while / in), I collected these coins.

_____ , I collected these coins.

(3) (his / judging / appearance / from), he seems to be rich.

_____ , he seems to be rich.

---

advice

2 (3)「コンピュータの電源を入れた」と「Eメールをチェックした」との時制のずれに注意する。

3 (1)分詞の否定語が not のときは分詞の前に置くが，never のときは分詞の前後どちらにも置くことができる。

12 | 受け身 ①

要点整理

❶ 受動態の基本

〈**be ＋他動詞の過去分詞（＋ by ＋動作主）**〉の形を用いる。

(1) **第3文型**(S ＋ V ＋ O)の場合

> My father *wrote* <u>this novel</u> last year.

　→ <u>This novel</u> **was written** by my father last year.

(2) **第4文型**(S ＋ V ＋ IO ＋ DO) の場合

> Mr. Tanaka *teaches* <u>us</u> <u>English</u> once a week.

　→ <u>We</u> **are taught** English by Mr. Tanaka once a week.

　→ <u>English</u> **is taught** (to) us by Mr. Tanaka once a week.

(3) **第5文型**(S ＋ V ＋ O ＋ C) の場合

> They *call* <u>the clock tower</u> Big Ben.

　→ <u>The clock tower</u> **is called** Big Ben. 〔動作主が不特定の場合は省略〕

check 1 次の各文を受動態を用いて書き換えよ。

(1) Mike washed the car yesterday.

_____

(2) My uncle gave me a dictionary on my birthday.

_____

(3) The parents named the baby John.

_____

❷ 受動態の慣用表現

(1) **感情を表す動詞**は，受動態で by 以外の前置詞を用いることが多い。

> He **was pleased** *with* the present.

(2) **特定の動詞**は，受動態で by 以外の前置詞を用いる。

> The story **is known** *to* everybody.

(3) **動作主が不特定**の場合は，by 〜以下を省略する。

> This bird is called 'blackbird' in English (*by people*).

check 2 次の各文の___に適当な前置詞を入れよ。

(1) I was interested _____ physics when I was at college.

(2) The ground was covered _____ snow.

(3) I was delighted _____ the news of his success.

1 次の各文の___に適当な前置詞を入れよ。

(1) Butter and cheese are made _____ milk.

(2) The girl was named _____ her grandmother. (a で始まる語)　　　　［実践女子大-改］

(3) We were caught _____ a shower on our way home.

2 次の各文の___に適当な語を入れ，受動態の文を完成させよ。

(1) The news surprised everybody.

→ Everybody _____ _____ _____ the news.

(2) My grade in English satisfied my father.

→ My father _____ _____ _____ my grade in English.

(3) Everyone in this city knows him well.

→ He _____ well _____ _____ everyone in this city.

(4) They speak Spanish in Mexico.

→ Spanish _____ _____ _____ _____.

3 次の各文を受動態を用いて書き換えよ。2種類できるものは2種類書くこと。

(1) A fireman saved the baby.

_____

(2) Bell invented the telephone in 1876.

_____

(3) My father painted the fence red.

_____

(4) They don't sell eggs at the store.

_____

(5) An old man told the children an amusing story.

_____

4 次の各文を能動態を用いて書き換えよ。

(1) We are taught English by Mr. Smith.

_____

(2) English is spoken in Australia.

_____

(3) He is called Honest John by everyone.

_____

(4) The baby was left alone by the parents.

_____

(5) John was scolded by his teacher for being late for school.

_____

advice
3 (5) 2種類の受動態が可能。

13 | 受け身 ②

🖝 要点整理

❶ いろいろな受動態

(1) **疑問文**の場合

> Did the boy paint this picture?

→ **Was** this picture **painted** by the boy?

> Who broke this vase?

→ *Who* **was** this vase **broken** *by*?

〔*By whom* **was** this vase **broken**?〕

(2) **助動詞を含む**場合

> You must send this letter at once.

→ This letter **must be sent** (by you) at once.

(3) **進行形**の場合

> A lot of workers are building a new bridge.

→ A new bridge **is being built** by a lot of workers.

(4) **群動詞**の場合

> A dump truck *ran over* the old man.

→ The old man **was run over** by a dump truck.

(5) **感覚動詞・使役動詞**の場合……原形不定詞は to 不定詞となる。

> We *saw* a stranger *go* into the room.

→ A stranger **was seen to *go*** into the room (by us).

(6) **目的語が that 節**の場合

> They say that she was a beauty in her youth.

→ **It is said that** she *was* a beauty in her youth.

→ **She is said to *have been*** a beauty in her youth.

check 1 次の各文を受動態を用いて書き換えよ。

(1) Who made this box?

_____

(2) Lucy will invite me to the party.

_____

(3) Tom saw her sing on the stage.

_____

(4) We paid no attention to his words.

_____

1 次の各文の適当な位置に，（　）内の語を入れよ。

(1) The large museum is built in the park.（being）

_____

(2) The boy is often made fun by his friends.（of）

_____

(3) A stranger was seen enter my house.（to）

_____

(4) The meeting will put off till next Sunday.（be）

_____

2 次の各文を受動態を用いて書き換えよ。

(1) They looked down on him as a liar.

_____

(2) The student has just done his homework.

_____

(3) Mother is cooking dinner in the kitchen.

_____

(4) When will the committee hold the meeting?

_____

(5) The children were watching their mother make a doll.

_____

☆ **3** 次の各組の英文がほぼ同じ内容になるように，____に適当な語を入れよ。

(1) ⎰ They say that Mr. White is leaving Japan next week.
⎱ ① _____ _____ _____ that Mr. White is leaving Japan next week.
② Mr. White _____ _____ _____ be leaving Japan next week.

(2) ⎰ We often hear him complain of his meals.
⎱ He is often _____ _____ _____ of his meals.

(3) ⎰ You must take good care of your health.
⎱ ① Your health _____ _____ _____ good care of.
② Good care _____ _____ _____ of your health.

4 日本語を参考に，____に適当な語を入れよ。

(1) あなたは外国人に話しかけられたことがありますか。　　　　　　　　　　　［東北学院大-改］

Have you ever been _____ _____ by a foreigner?

(2) この魚は悪くなる前に食べるべきだ。

This fish should _____ _____ before it goes bad.

(3) ジョージは母親に皿洗いをさせられた。

George was _____ _____ do the dishes by his mother.

(4) その少年はクラスの生徒全員に笑われた。

The boy was _____ _____ by all the students in his class.

14 | 比　較 ①

🖐 要点整理

❶ 基本的な比較表現

　２つあるいは，それ以上のものを比較して述べるとき，**形容詞・副詞の原級**，**比較級**，**最上級**を用いて表す。**規則変化**と**不規則変化**の２通りがある。

check 1 次の各文の（　）内の語を適当な形にせよ。なお，変える必要のない語はそのまま書くこと。

(1) Which is (big), this apple or that?　　　　　　　　　＿＿＿＿＿＿

(2) Yui plays the piano (well) than Aki.　　　　　　　　＿＿＿＿＿＿

(3) Tokyo is the (large) city in Japan.　　　　　　　　　＿＿＿＿＿＿

(4) My brother can speak English (fluently) of all.　　　＿＿＿＿＿＿

(5) Nothing is as (exciting) as American football.　　　＿＿＿＿＿＿

❷ 原級・比較級・最上級の転換

　同じ語の**原級・比較級・最上級**を用いて，**同じ意味**を表すことができる。

check 2 次の各組の英文がほぼ同じ内容になるように，＿＿に適当な語を入れよ。

(1)
① Nothing is as ＿＿＿＿＿ ＿＿＿＿＿ time.
② ＿＿＿＿＿ is ＿＿＿＿＿ valuable than anything else.
③ Time is ＿＿＿＿＿ ＿＿＿＿＿ valuable thing.

(2)
① Mt. Fuji is ＿＿＿＿＿ ＿＿＿＿＿ mountain in Japan.
② Mt. Fuji is ＿＿＿＿＿ than ＿＿＿＿＿ other mountain in Japan.
③ ＿＿＿＿＿ other mountain in Japan is as high as Mt. Fuji.
④ ＿＿＿＿＿ other mountain in Japan is ＿＿＿＿＿ than Mt. Fuji.

---

1 次の各語の比較級，最上級を書け。

(1) diligent ＿＿＿＿＿ ＿＿＿＿＿ 　　(2) happy ＿＿＿＿＿ ＿＿＿＿＿

(3) carefully ＿＿＿＿＿ ＿＿＿＿＿ 　　(4) thin ＿＿＿＿＿ ＿＿＿＿＿

(5) slowly ＿＿＿＿＿ ＿＿＿＿＿ 　　(6) little ＿＿＿＿＿ ＿＿＿＿＿

(7) few ＿＿＿＿＿ ＿＿＿＿＿ 　　(8) much ＿＿＿＿＿ ＿＿＿＿＿

(9) many ＿＿＿＿＿ ＿＿＿＿＿ 　　(10) bad ＿＿＿＿＿ ＿＿＿＿＿

(11) ill ＿＿＿＿＿ ＿＿＿＿＿ 　　(12) good ＿＿＿＿＿ ＿＿＿＿＿

(13) well ＿＿＿＿＿ ＿＿＿＿＿ 　　(14) far ＿＿＿＿＿ ＿＿＿＿＿

(15) late ＿＿＿＿＿ ＿＿＿＿＿

2 次の各文の（　）内の語を最も適当な形にせよ。

(1) Which knife cuts (well), this or that?　　　　　＿＿＿＿＿＿

(2) To know oneself is (important) than anything else.　　　　　＿＿＿＿＿＿

(3) This dress is the (cheap) of the three.　　　　　＿＿＿＿＿＿

(4) The (late) half of this book is very interesting.　　　　　＿＿＿＿＿＿

(5) The sun sets (late) in summer than in winter.　　　　　＿＿＿＿＿＿

☆ **3** 次の各組の英文がほぼ同じ内容になるように，＿＿に適当な語を入れよ。

(1) ⎰ Nothing is as pleasant as traveling.
　　⎱ Nothing is ＿＿＿＿＿ ＿＿＿＿＿ than traveling.

(2) ⎰ Gold is the most precious of all metals.
　　⎱ Gold is ＿＿＿＿＿ precious than ＿＿＿＿＿ other metal.

(3) ⎰ The Mississippi is the longest river in America.
　　⎱ ＿＿＿＿＿ other river in America is ＿＿＿＿＿ than the Mississippi.

(4) ⎰ I have never heard such an interesting story as this.
　　⎱ This is the ＿＿＿＿＿ ＿＿＿＿＿ story that I have ＿＿＿＿＿ heard.

☆ **4** 次の各文を文法的に正しい英文にせよ。

(1) It is very colder today than yesterday.

＿＿＿＿＿＿＿＿＿＿＿＿＿＿＿＿＿＿＿＿＿＿＿＿＿＿＿＿＿＿＿＿

(2) He looks more ill than yesterday.

＿＿＿＿＿＿＿＿＿＿＿＿＿＿＿＿＿＿＿＿＿＿＿＿＿＿＿＿＿＿＿＿

(3) Ted is the smartest boy of our class.

＿＿＿＿＿＿＿＿＿＿＿＿＿＿＿＿＿＿＿＿＿＿＿＿＿＿＿＿＿＿＿＿

(4) Bob is the tallest of the twin brothers.

＿＿＿＿＿＿＿＿＿＿＿＿＿＿＿＿＿＿＿＿＿＿＿＿＿＿＿＿＿＿＿＿

5 日本語を参考に，（　）内の語句を並べかえよ。

(1) こんなおいしいリンゴを今まで食べたことがない。　　　　［東京経済大］

This is (ever / wonderful / have / I / apple / the most) tasted.

This is ＿＿＿＿＿＿＿＿＿＿＿＿＿＿＿＿＿＿＿＿＿＿ tasted.

(2) この国は現在どの国よりも多くの車を生産している。　　　　［駒澤大-改］

This country is now (other / cars / country / than / producing / any / more).

This country is now ＿＿＿＿＿＿＿＿＿＿＿＿＿＿＿＿＿＿＿＿＿＿.

(3) この写真では，彼女は実際よりずっと若く見える。　　　　［東京家政大］

This photo (much / look / she / than / younger / makes / her / really is).

This photo ＿＿＿＿＿＿＿＿＿＿＿＿＿＿＿＿＿＿＿＿＿＿＿＿＿＿.

15 | 比　較 ②

要点整理

❶ 原級の慣用表現

as ～ as one can = as ～ as possible「できるだけ～」，倍数の表現，**not so much A as B**「A というよりむしろ B」などがある。

check 1 日本語を参考に，＿＿に適当な語を入れよ。

(1) 君はできるだけすぐに帰って来なければならない。

You must come back as ＿＿＿＿＿＿ ＿＿＿＿＿＿ you can.

(2) オーストラリアは日本の約 20 倍の広さだ。

Australia is about twenty ＿＿＿＿＿＿ as ＿＿＿＿＿＿ ＿＿＿＿＿＿ Japan.

(3) 彼は教師というよりむしろ学者だ。

He is ＿＿＿＿＿＿ ＿＿＿＿＿＿ ＿＿＿＿＿＿ a teacher as a scholar.

❷ 比較級の慣用表現

the ＋比較級～，the ＋比較級 ...「～すればするほど，ますます…だ」，**no more than = only, not more than = at most, no less than = as much〔many〕as, not less than = at least** などがある。

check 2 次の各組の英文がほぼ同じ内容になるように，＿＿に適当な語を入れよ。

(1) {
As we went up higher, it became colder.
＿＿＿＿＿＿ ＿＿＿＿＿＿ we went up, ＿＿＿＿＿＿ ＿＿＿＿＿＿ it became.
}

(2) {
My father has not less than a thousand books.
My father has ＿＿＿＿＿＿ ＿＿＿＿＿＿ a thousand books.
}

❸ 最上級の慣用表現

the ＋ second〔third ... 〕＋最上級「2〔3 …〕番目に～」，**at least**「少なくとも」，**at most**「多くとも」，**at one's best**「最盛期で」などがある。

check 3 次の各文の（　）内の語を最も適当な形にせよ。

(1) K2 is the second (high) mountain in the world. ＿＿＿＿＿＿

(2) The plum trees will be at their (good) in a few days. ＿＿＿＿＿＿

(3) The Browns enjoy traveling abroad at (little) twice a year. ＿＿＿＿＿＿

❹ than ではなく to を用いる比較級

be superior to ～「～より優れている」，**be inferior to ～**「～より劣っている」，**be senior to ～**「～より年上である」，**be junior to ～**「～より年下である」，**prefer A to B**「B よりも A が好きだ」などがある。

☆ **1** 次の各文を，下線部に注意して，日本語に直せ。

(1) The Ishikari is the third longest river in Japan.

( )

(2) That player was at his best in the game yesterday.

( )

(3) My room is half as large as my sister's.

( )

(4) The questions in the test were getting more and more difficult.

( )

(5) My suitcase weighs at least fifteen kilograms.

( )

(6) She is junior to her boyfriend by three years.

( )

(7) This is the best steak that I have ever had.

( )

(8) The younger you are, the easier it is to get used to something.

( )

(9) He is not so much a pianist as a composer.

( )

(10) It will take me not more than two hours to finish writing this paper.

( )

2 次の各組の英文がほぼ同じ内容になるように，____に適当な語を入れよ。

(1) { I like watching baseball better than playing it.
    { I _____ watching baseball to _____ it.

(2) { Mt. Everest is the highest mountain in the world.
    { Mt. Everest is _____ than any other _____ in the world.

(3) { He ate lunch as quickly as possible.
    { He ate lunch as quickly as_____ _____.

(4) { We stayed in Kyoto for only two days.
    { We stayed in Kyoto for _____ _____ than two days.

---

advice ....

2 (1) like A better than B = prefer A to B

16 | 関係詞 ①

🖐 要点整理

❶ 関係代名詞と先行詞

　　関係代名詞……２つの節をつなぐ**接続詞**と**代名詞の役割**を同時に果たす。関係詞の導く節が修飾する語を**先行詞**という。

> *The woman* **who** lives next door is a doctor.〔先行詞＝人〕

> Did you see *the letter* **which** came today?〔先行詞＝物・動物〕

> Mary is *the prettiest girl* **that** I have ever seen.〔先行詞＝人・動物・物〕

　(all, the only, 最上級などのついた先行詞とともによく用いられる。)

> **What** I need is a good sleep.〔先行詞を含む what ＝ the thing(s) which 〜〕

check 1 次の各文の＿＿に適当な関係代名詞を入れよ。

(1) ＿＿＿＿＿＿ you said and ＿＿＿＿＿＿ you did were not the same.

(2) Your father is the best person ＿＿＿＿＿＿ can advise you on the matters.

(3) What's the name of the girl ＿＿＿＿＿＿ just came in?

❷ 関係代名詞と前置詞

　　関係代名詞(whom, which)が**前置詞の目的語**になるとき，前置詞が関係代名詞の直前に置かれる場合と，関係代名詞節の最後に置かれる場合がある。

> This is the office **in which** *my father works*.

　＝ This is the office (**which**〔**that**〕) *my father works* **in**.

check 2 次の各文を文法的に正しい英文にせよ。

(1) The man you spoke the other day is my boss.

＿＿＿＿＿＿＿＿＿＿＿＿＿＿＿＿＿＿＿＿＿＿＿＿＿＿＿＿

(2) Mathematics is the subject I am interested.

＿＿＿＿＿＿＿＿＿＿＿＿＿＿＿＿＿＿＿＿＿＿＿＿＿＿＿＿

❸ その他の関係詞

　　the same 〜 as …，**such 〜 as …**，**but**(関係詞＋ not)などがある。

> He has **the same** dictionary **as** I have.

check 3 次の各文を日本語に直せ。

(1) Read only such books as will help you.

　(　　　　　　　　　　　　　　　　　　　　　　　　　　　　　　　)

(2) There is no rule but has exceptions.

　(　　　　　　　　　　　　　　　　　　　　　　　　　　　　　　　)

1 次の各組の文を関係代名詞を用いて1つの文にせよ。

(1) The woman was a Chinese. / I met her at the airport.

_____

(2) The girl is Jessica. / I believed she was Mark's girlfriend.

_____

(3) This is the restaurant. / I once talked about it.

_____

2 次の各文の____に適当な関係代名詞を入れよ。

(1) I don't like people _____ lose their temper easily.

(2) This is the boy _____ I think is the smartest in the class.

(3) The lady to _____ I introduced you is my aunt.

(4) We always buy the best materials _____ we can find.

(5) The house _____ is for sale is at the end of the street.

(6) This book is exactly _____ I wanted.   [センター試験]

(7) She is the girl _____ bicycle was stolen.

(8) The captain was the last person _____ left the sinking ship.

3 次の各文を文法的に正しい英文にせよ。

(1) I will show you the computer which I bought it yesterday.

_____

(2) He is the teacher from him I borrowed this book yesterday.

_____

(3) Buy it back from the man you sold it.

_____

(4) Look at the boy and his dog which are running after a fox.

_____

(5) He is not that he used to be.

_____

4 次の各組の英文がほぼ同じ内容になるように，____に適当な語を入れよ。

(1) { Look at that man with gray hair.
    { Look at that man _____ _____ is gray.

(2) { You only have to stay here.
    { The only thing _____ _____ have to do is to stay here.

advice
3 (5)関係代名詞 that の先行詞がないことに注目。

17 | 関係詞 ②

要点整理

❶ 関係副詞

　　関係副詞……節と節を結びつける**接続詞**と**副詞の役割**を果たす。〈前置詞＋関係代名詞〉に置きかえられることが多い。

> Saturday is *the day* **when**(= *on which*) I don't work.
> Do you remember *the hotel* **where**(= *at which*) we stayed?
> His laziness is *the reason* **why**(= *for which*) he failed.
> Tell me **how**(= *the way in which*) you learned to speak Chinese.

check 1 次の各文の＿＿に適当な関係副詞を入れよ。

(1) Sunday is the day ＿＿＿＿＿＿ I am least busy.

(2) There is no reason ＿＿＿＿＿＿ you should stay here.

(3) The dog sat in the shade ＿＿＿＿＿＿ it was cool.

❷ 限定用法と継続用法

(1) **限定用法**……関係詞の前に**コンマがない**。先行詞を限定的に修飾。
> He has two sons **who** became doctors.
　（彼には，医者になった息子が２人いる。）……息子は３人以上の可能性もある。

(2) **継続用法**……関係詞の前に**コンマがある**。先行詞の補足説明を付加。
> He has two sons**, who** became doctors.
　（彼には息子が２人いて，彼らは医者になった。）……息子は２人だけ。

check 2 次の各文を日本語に直せ。

(1) Mozart, whose music you have been listening to, is my favorite composer.
　（　　　　　　　　　　　　　　　　　　　　　　　　　　　　　　　　　　）

(2) My vacation, when I can get some rest, is coming soon.
　（　　　　　　　　　　　　　　　　　　　　　　　　　　　　　　　　　　）

❸ 複合関係詞

　　whoever(= anyone who 〜) , **whomever**(= anyone whom 〜) , **whichever**(= any one 〔ones〕 that 〜) , **whatever**(= anything that 〜) , **wherever**(= at〔to〕 any place where 〜) , **whenever**(= at any time when 〜) ,　**however**

check 3 次の各文の＿＿に適当な複合関係詞を入れよ。

(1) Take ＿＿＿＿＿＿ book you like.

(2) ＿＿＿＿＿＿ broke the window must pay for it.

1 次の各文の＿＿に適当な関係副詞を入れよ。

(1) I don't know the reason ＿＿＿＿＿＿ Ted can't come with us.

(2) That's the shop ＿＿＿＿＿＿ he bought the gloves.

(3) She wants to live in the country ＿＿＿＿＿＿ the weather is mild.

(4) 1945 was the year ＿＿＿＿＿＿ the Second World War ended.

(5) Her cat is missing —— that's ＿＿＿＿＿＿ she looks so sad.

☆ **2** 次の各文の＿＿に適当な関係詞を入れよ。

(1) This is the very book ＿＿＿＿＿＿ I have been looking for.

(2) John is a man ＿＿＿＿＿＿ work takes him abroad a lot.

(3) Let's find a quiet place ＿＿＿＿＿＿ we can talk.

(4) The subject ＿＿＿＿＿＿ he likes best is chemistry.

(5) Her father, ＿＿＿＿＿＿ died of cancer, had been a heavy smoker.

(6) I remembered the place ＿＿＿＿＿＿ I had left my books.

(7) This is the house in ＿＿＿＿＿＿ Shakespeare was born.

(8) He doesn't take enough exercise —— that's ＿＿＿＿＿＿ he's too fat.

3 日本語を参考に，（　）内の語句を並べかえよ。

(1) このようにして私は彼と知り合いになったのです。　　　　　　　　　　　　　［城西大］

(came / him / how / I / is / know / this / to).

＿＿＿＿＿＿＿＿＿＿＿＿＿＿＿＿＿＿＿＿＿＿＿＿＿＿＿＿＿＿＿＿＿＿＿＿.

(2) 彼らはハネムーンで滞在予定のホテルに到着した。

They arrived at the hotel (for / staying / their / they / were / where) honeymoon.

They arrived at the hotel ＿＿＿＿＿＿＿＿＿＿＿＿＿＿＿＿＿＿＿＿＿ honeymoon.

4 次の各文の＿＿に下から適当な複合関係詞を選んで入れよ。ただし，同じ語を2度使わないこと。

(1) Some children eat ＿＿＿＿＿＿ they are hungry.

(2) ＿＿＿＿＿＿ wants the book may have it.

(3) Sit ＿＿＿＿＿＿ you like.

(4) I will do ＿＿＿＿＿＿ you ask me to do.

〔whoever, whenever, wherever, whatever〕

18 | 仮定法

要点整理

❶ 仮定法の基本用法

(1) **仮定法未来**……実際に起こる可能性が少ないと思われる仮定，また **were to** を用いれば純粋な仮定を表す。

$$\text{If } S + \begin{Bmatrix} \textbf{should} \\ \textbf{were to} \end{Bmatrix} + 原形\sim, \ S + \begin{Bmatrix} \textbf{would, should} \\ \textbf{might, could} \end{Bmatrix} + 原形 ....$$

(2) **仮定法過去**……現在の事実に反する仮定を表す。

$$\text{If } S + \begin{Bmatrix} \textbf{were〔was〕} \\ \textbf{過去形} \end{Bmatrix} \sim, \ S + \begin{Bmatrix} \textbf{would, should} \\ \textbf{might, could} \end{Bmatrix} + 原形 ....$$

(3) **仮定法過去完了**……過去の事実に反する仮定を表す。

$$\text{If } S + \textbf{had} + 過去分詞\sim, \ S + \begin{Bmatrix} \textbf{would, should} \\ \textbf{might, could} \end{Bmatrix} + \textbf{have} + 過去分詞 ....$$

check 1 次の各文の（　）内の語を最も適当な形にせよ。

(1) If I (be) in your place, I would buy the car at once. ＿＿＿＿＿＿

(2) If you (come) a little later, you might have missed the bus. ＿＿＿＿＿＿

(3) If I (be) to die, what would become of my family? ＿＿＿＿＿＿

(4) What would you do if you (shall) fail? ＿＿＿＿＿＿

❷ 仮定法特有の表現

> He speaks **as if** he **knew** everything. 「まるで〜 かのように」

> **I wish** I **had** enough money. 「〜 であればよいのに」

> **It is** (**high**) **time** you **went** to bed. 「もう〜する時間だ」

> **If it were not for 〜 / If it had not been for 〜** 「〜がなければ」
> **But for 〜**, **Without 〜** も同じ意味を表す。

> **Were I** young, I **could** go abroad. 〔倒置による If の省略〕

> I **ordered** that he (**should**) **go** to hospital.
> 〔仮定法現在：命令・提案などを表す that 節内では，〈(should ＋)原形〉を用いる〕

check 2 次の各文の＿＿＿に適当な語を入れよ。

(1) ＿＿＿＿＿ for your help, I could not accomplish this project.

(2) ＿＿＿＿＿ you come earlier, you could have met her.

(3) She looks ＿＿＿＿＿ if she had been ill for a long time.

1 次の各文の＿＿に適当な語を入れ，仮定法の文を完成させよ。

(1) As he doesn't have enough money, he can't buy a new car.

If he ＿＿＿＿＿＿ enough money, he ＿＿＿＿＿＿ buy a new car.

(2) As I am not a bird, I won't fly in the sky.

If I ＿＿＿＿＿＿ a bird, I ＿＿＿＿＿＿ fly in the sky.

(3) I missed the bus, so I couldn't be in time.

If I hadn't ＿＿＿＿＿＿ the bus, I ＿＿＿＿＿＿ have been in time.

(4) As I was ill, I couldn't play golf with them. 〔実践女子大-改〕

If I ＿＿＿＿＿＿ not been ill, I ＿＿＿＿＿＿ ＿＿＿＿＿＿ played golf with them.

(5) As it rained a lot yesterday, we can't ride a bike.

If it ＿＿＿＿＿＿ not ＿＿＿＿＿＿ a lot yesterday, we ＿＿＿＿＿＿ ride a bike.

☆ **2** 次の各組の英文がほぼ同じ内容になるように，＿＿に適当な語を入れよ。

(1) { Without your advice, we would have failed.

If it ＿＿＿＿＿＿ ＿＿＿＿＿＿ ＿＿＿＿＿＿ ＿＿＿＿＿＿ your advice, we would have failed.

(2) { I am sorry that I cannot go to the concert.

I ＿＿＿＿＿＿ I ＿＿＿＿＿＿ go to the concert.

(3) { Our English teacher speaks English like an Englishman.

Our English teacher speaks English ＿＿＿＿＿＿ ＿＿＿＿＿＿ he ＿＿＿＿＿＿ an Englishman.

(4) { As I was not there, I didn't speak to him.

＿＿＿＿＿＿ I ＿＿＿＿＿＿ there, I would have spoken to him.

(5) { We must leave now.

It is high ＿＿＿＿＿＿ we ＿＿＿＿＿＿.

3 次の各文の（ ）内の語句を並べかえよ。

(1) I (the book / wish / I / before / read / had) the examination. 〔日本大-改〕

I ＿＿＿＿＿＿＿＿＿＿＿＿＿＿＿＿＿＿＿＿＿＿＿＿ the examination.

(2) Her teacher (proposed / every day / she / that / English / study) . 〔杏林大-改〕

Her teacher ＿＿＿＿＿＿＿＿＿＿＿＿＿＿＿＿＿＿＿＿＿＿＿＿.

(3) If I had not (have / had / attended / a cold / the meeting / I could / ,). 〔札幌大-改〕

If I had not ＿＿＿＿＿＿＿＿＿＿＿＿＿＿＿＿＿＿＿＿＿＿＿＿.

(4) Were (for / not / support / your / it), our company couldn't survive.

Were ＿＿＿＿＿＿＿＿＿＿＿＿＿＿＿＿＿＿＿＿ , our company couldn't survive.

advice --
1 (5)従属節は過去の事柄，主節は現在の事柄であることに注意。

19 | 否 定

解答 ▶ 別冊p.16

🖐 要点整理

❶ 基本的な否定語

not は特定の語句を否定する**語否定**と，文を否定する**文否定**がある。また，not が**否定文**の役割を果たすことがある。**no** は主に**名詞の前**に置いて**否定**を表す。

check 1 次の各文を文法的に正しい英文にせよ。

(1) Anyone cannot solve this problem.

_____

(2) I think it will not rain tomorrow.

_____

(3) The doctor advised him to not eat too much.

_____

(4) "It's still snowing. Will the plane take off on time?" "I'm not afraid."

_____

❷ 部分否定

every，**all**，**both**，**always**，**necessarily** などの前に**否定語**がつくと，全体でなく**部分否定**となる。

check 2 次の各組の文を，意味の違いに注意して，日本語に直せ。

(1)
　① I don't know both of your brothers.
　　(　　　　　　　　　　　　　　　　　　　　　　　　　　)
　② I don't know either of your brothers.
　　(　　　　　　　　　　　　　　　　　　　　　　　　　　)

(2)
　① Mike is not always late for class.
　　(　　　　　　　　　　　　　　　　　　　　　　　　　　)
　② Mike is never late for class.
　　(　　　　　　　　　　　　　　　　　　　　　　　　　　)

❸ 準否定語

〈**few ＋ 可算名詞**〉，〈**little ＋ 不可算名詞**〉，**hardly・scarcely**「ほとんど～ない」，**rarely・seldom**「めったに～しない」は**否定の意味**を表す。

check 3 次の各文の適当な位置に，（　）内の語を入れよ。

(1) There is hope of his success. (little)

_____

(2) Good fortune comes in succession. (rarely)

_____

(3) She is lonely. She has friends. (few)

_____

(4) I am so tired that I can walk. (hardly)

_____

1 次の各文を，部分否定は全体否定に，全体否定は部分否定に書き換えよ。

(1) I can't speak both English and French.

_____

(2) Not all of my students work hard.

_____

(3) I don't understand any of these questions.

_____

☆ **2** 次の各組の英文がほぼ同じ内容になるように，＿＿に適当な語を入れよ。

(1) { There is no rule but has exceptions.
{ There is no rule that _____ _____ have exceptions.

(2) { There are no mistakes in your composition.
{ Your composition is _____ _____ mistakes.

(3) { He is a man who never keeps his promise.
{ He is the _____ person to keep his promise.

(4) { You must be very careful when you drive a car.
{ You can _____ be _____ careful in driving a car.

(5) { A cold winter will come before long.
{ It will _____ be long _____ a cold winter comes.

(6) { Whenever I hear this song, I remember my happy days.
{ I _____ hear this song _____ remembering my happy days.

3 次の各文の( )内に下から適当なものを選び，記号で答えよ。

(1) We could ( ) help laughing at this foolish deed.

　　ア but　　**イ** not　　**ウ** only

(2) ( ) but love can save the world.

　　ア All　　**イ** Anything　　**ウ** Nothing

(3) He was unable to attend the party, ( ) did he want to. 〔摂南大-改〕

　　ア either　　**イ** nor　　**ウ** so

advice
2 (1) but は否定を含む関係代名詞。
3 (1) cannot help ～ing ＝ cannot but ＋原形

41

20 | 接続詞

要点整理

❶ 等位接続詞

語・句・節を対等の関係で結びつける **and，but，or，nor，so，for** などである。

check 1 次の各文の＿＿に適当な接続詞を入れよ。

(1) I don't like vegetables, ＿＿＿＿＿ does my father.

(2) Hurry up, ＿＿＿＿＿ you will be late for class.

(3) My watch is very old, ＿＿＿＿＿ it keeps good time.

(4) Get up early, ＿＿＿＿＿ you'll be in time for the first train.

❷ 従位接続詞

名詞節を導く **that，if，whether，** 副詞節を導く **when，till，because，if，though，unless，as long as，as，before，after** などである。

check 2 次の各文の＿＿に適当な接続詞を入れよ。

(1) The news ＿＿＿＿＿ he was still alive surprised us.

(2) Brush your teeth ＿＿＿＿＿ you go to bed.

(3) It's doubtful ＿＿＿＿＿ you'll finish the work for yourself.

(4) I went out last night ＿＿＿＿＿ I had a little fever.

❸ 相関接続詞

both A and B「AとBの両方とも」，**either A or B**「AかBのどちらか」，**neither A nor B**「AとBのどちらも～でない」，**not only A but (also) B ＝ B as well as A**「Aだけでなく B も」，**not A but B**「AでなくB」などである。

check 3 次の各文の＿＿に適当な語を入れよ。

(1) To keep early hours is not only economical ＿＿＿＿＿ good for our health.

(2) ＿＿＿＿＿ he nor you are the right person for the post.

(3) John as ＿＿＿＿＿ as his friends was injured in the game.

(4) It was not a CD ＿＿＿＿＿ a DVD that I bought.

(5) ＿＿＿＿＿ you or your brother should come soon.

1 次の各文の（ ）内から適当なものを選べ。

(1) Ask him (that，if，because) he will drive us home.

(2) (Since，Though，Before) you walk across the street, look to the right and to the left.

(3) It has been years (before，since，when) I saw him last.

(4) (As，Though，If) he grew older, he became less active.

(5) Start at once, (or，and，but) you will be able to catch up with him.

(6) Either my husband (nor，and，or) I have to stay home tomorrow.　　　　　[東京国際大-改]

(7) (As，Though，If) he is only four years old, he is quite tall.

(8) Everybody knows the fact (that，if，whether) the earth is round.

☆ **2** 日本語を参考に，（ ）内の語句を並べかえよ。ただし，不足する１語を加えること。

(1) 彼女は私たちに本だけでなくＣＤもくれた。

(she / a book / as / as / gave us / a CD).

_____.

(2) あなたが座れるように，席をもう１つとっておきました。

(you / been / seat / I've / that / keeping / another) can sit.

_____ can sit.

(3) カナダでは英語もフランス語も話される。

(English / in / are / both / spoken / French) Canada.

_____ Canada.

(4) 話さないかぎり，彼女は賢く見える。

She (doesn't / long / looks / she / as / smart / speak).

She _____.

(5) 丈夫な胃を持っていないのなら，その国で水道水を飲まないほうがいい。

(you / you / a strong stomach / in / have / not / tap water / drink / had better / ,) that country.

_____

_____ that country.

☆ **3** 次の各文の＿＿に適当な接続詞を入れよ。

(1) It will not be long _____ we can travel in space.

(2) The trouble is _____ he has lost his passport.

(3) Young _____ he was, he was equal to the post.

(4) Even _____ you don't help us, we will do it for ourselves.

(5) A book is not always a good book just _____ it is written by a famous writer.

[センター試験]

21 | 名詞・冠詞

要点整理

❶ 可算名詞と不可算名詞

(1) **可算名詞**……**普通名詞・集合名詞**。単数・複数の区別があり，a〔an〕，a few，many など数を表す語句で修飾される。

集合名詞の種類

ⓐ 単数と複数の両形があり，文脈によって，単数形で複数扱いをすることがある。
…… family，team，audience
例 My family *are* all early risers.

ⓑ 常に単数形・複数扱い。…… police，cattle

(2) **不可算名詞**……**物質名詞・抽象名詞・固有名詞**。一般に単数と複数の区別はなく，単数扱いにする。a〔an〕はつけない。

日本語では可算名詞扱いだが，英語では不可算名詞…… furniture，advice，baggage
物質名詞の数え方…… a **cup** of coffee，a **bottle** of milk，a **cake** of soap，
two **sheets** of paper など。

check 1 次の各文を文法的に正しい英文にせよ。

(1) The police is investigating the murder.

_____

(2) We have collected a lot of informations on the matter.

_____

(3) There are not much furniture in his room.

_____

❷ 不定冠詞と定冠詞

(1) **不定冠詞**…… **a〔an〕**(= one)は**可算名詞の単数形**の前につける。

＞We are of **an**(= the same) age.

＞**An**(= One) apple **a**(= per) day keeps the doctor away.

(2) **定冠詞**…… **the** はどの名詞の前にもつき，単数・複数は問わない。

＞I saw *a man*. **The** *man* was our new teacher.〔既出の名詞の前〕

＞He patted me on **the** shoulder.〔慣用……所有格の代用〕

check 2 次の各文の____に適当な冠詞を入れよ。

(1) What is _____ first day of the week?

(2) Can you come and see us in _____ hour?

(3) _____ moon goes round _____ earth.

☆ **1** 次の各文の（　）内から適当なものを選べ。

(1) We have a lot of (work，works) to do today.

(2) Can we have two (glass，glasses) of orange juice, please? ［金沢工業大］

(3) All of his money (was，were) spent on gambling.

(4) The foreigner was carrying a lot of (baggage，baggages).

(5) There was (a fire，fire) in the neighborhood last night.

(6) It is said that the Japanese (is，are) a hardworking people.

(7) Let me give you (a bit of advice，a few advices). ［大阪学院大］

(8) The rich (is，are) not always happy.

2 次の各文の必要な位置に適当な冠詞を入れ，全文を書け。

(1) We usually take walk after dinner.

_____

(2) I can't do two things at time.

_____

(3) A stranger caught me by hand.

_____

(4) How often do you go to the barber's month?

_____

(5) He is one of smartest students in our class.

_____

(6) Would you mind opening window?

_____

3 次の各文の＿＿に下から適当なものを選んで入れよ。ただし，同じ語を２度使わないこと。

(1) a _____ of tea　　　　(2) a _____ of news

(3) a _____ of beer　　　　(4) a _____ of paper

(5) a _____ of soap　　　　(6) a _____ of bread

〔loaf，cake，bottle，cup，piece，sheet〕

4 次の各文の（　）内から適当なものを選べ。

(1) We solved the problem with (ease，easily).

(2) I like playing baseball. It's a lot of (fun，funny) to play baseball.

(3) I have never read any (Shakespeare，Shakespeares).

(4) It is of no (important，importance) to us.

(5) My mother often reads a piece of (poem，poetry) to me.

要点整理

❶ 人称代名詞

(1) **we**, **you**, **they** などは**不特定の「一般の人々」**を表すことがある。
> "**We** have little snow here in winter. Do **you** have much in London?"

(2) **it** は，**時・天候・明暗・距離**などを表す文の主語となる。また，**形式主語，形式目的語，強調構文の主語**となる。
> What time is **it** by your watch? 〔時〕
> **It** is you *that* are to blame. 〔強調構文〕

(3) **所有代名詞**
> This watch of **mine** is very expensive.

(4) **再帰代名詞**
> We enjoyed **ourselves** at the party. 〔再帰用法〕
> The prime minister **himself** came to our town. 〔強調用法〕

check 1 次の各文の（　）内から適当なものを選べ。

(1) The lady with a hat on is an old friend of (my，mine).

(2) Please help (you，yourself) to the cookies.

(3) (It，That) cost me ten dollars to get the ticket.

❷ 指示代名詞

(1) **前出の語の繰り返しを避ける that〔those〕**
> *The population* of Japan is larger than **that** of Korea.

(2) **those who ～の形で** people who ～「～する人々」の意味で用いる。
> **Those** (**who** were) present were all men.

(3) **前文の内容の一部を受ける so, such**
> Will it be fine tomorrow? — I hope **so**.
> He is a great statesman and is respected as **such**.

check 2 次の各文の（　）内の語句を並べかえよ。

(1) His behavior is (that / of / not / gentleman / a).
His behavior is _____.

(2) Heaven helps (who / those / themselves / help).
Heaven helps _____.

☆ **1** 次の各文を文法的に正しい英文にせよ。

(1) My sister always looks at her in the mirror.

_____

(2) The climate of this country is like Japan.

_____

(3) My room is not as large as you.

_____

(4) This my album is the only thing to show you.

_____

(5) "Hello. I am Mike Smith speaking."

_____

2 次の各文の____に下から適当なものを選んで入れよ。ただし，同じ語を2度使わないこと。

(1) "Do _____ speak Spanish in Mexico?" "Yes, I think so."

(2) _____ is believed that French food is the best in the world.

(3) He made up his mind to carry out the task for _____.

(4) Tom and Lucy enjoyed _____ at the party last night.

(5) Let's go out and celebrate, shall _____?

(6) Come and sit here, will _____?

〔themselves，you，this，they，himself，we，oneself，it，that〕

3 日本語を参考に，____に適当な語を入れよ。

(1) どうぞくつろいでください。

Please make _____ at _____.

(2) 食べることが好きな人はよく，料理に挑戦する。

_____ who like to eat often try to cook.（Tで始まる語）

(3) 近ごろ，私は毎週末，息子と釣りを楽しみます。

_____ days I enjoy fishing with my son every weekend.

4 次の各組の英文がほぼ同じ内容になるように，____に適当な語を入れよ。

(1) { He is said to be honest.
　　{ _____ is said _____ he is honest.

(2) { The woman had to finish the work alone.
　　{ The woman had to finish the work by _____.

(3) { In Japan, we have a lot of rain in June.
　　{ In Japan, _____ rains a _____ in June.

23 | 代名詞 ②

月　　日

解答 ▶ 別冊pp.19-20

要点整理

❶ 不定代名詞

不定の数・量を表す代名詞であるが，多くは**形容詞**としても用いられる。

(1) **one** は**前出の可算名詞**を受ける。また「**一般の人**」を表すことがある。

> I've lost my camera. I must buy **one** (＝ a camera).

> **One** should keep **one's** promise.

(2) **another** と **other**

> This dress is too expensive. Show me **another**. 「もう１つ別の服」

> I have two sons; **one** is a doctor, and **the other** is a lawyer.

「（２人のうち）１人と残りの１人」

> I have three sons; **one** lives in London, and **the others** in Tokyo.

「（３人のうち）１人と残りの２人（全部）」

> **Some** people came by car, and **others** came on foot.

「（不特定多数のうち）ある人たちとまたある人たち」

(3) **some**……肯定文，または肯定の答えを期待する疑問文に用いる。

> Won't you have **some** more coffee? 〔勧誘〕

> **any**……否定文・疑問文に用いる。〈any ＋単数名詞〉で肯定文に用いる。

> Do you have **any** questions? — Yes, I have some.

> **Any** bus from here *stops* at Shibuya. 「どんな〜でも」

(4) > **All** of us *are* more or less selfish. 〔数… 複数扱い〕

> **All** of the food *has* gone. 〔量… 単数扱い〕

> **Both** of his parents *are* excellent singers. 〔複数扱い〕

(5) **each**，**every** は**単数扱い**。**either**，**neither**（either の否定形）は原則として**単数扱い**だが，〈either〔neither〕of ＋複数（代）名詞〉は，口語では複数扱いすることもある。

> **Every** student *has* to do his or her best. 〔形容詞用法のみ，単数扱い〕

> I don't like **either** of the two men.

> **Neither** of the stories *was*〔*were*〕true.

check 1 次の各文の（　）内から適当な語句を選べ。

(1)（Each，Every）of the three boys has got a prize.

(2) "Do you want a ball-point pen?" "Yes, I want (one，it)."

(3) I have two bags; (one，another) is large and (the other，another) is medium size.

1 次の各文の____に the other，others，another，the others のうち適当なものを，それぞれ
１つずつ入れよ。

(1) Would you like _____ piece of cake?

(2) She has five dogs; one is black, and _____ are white.

(3) Some believe in the existence of God and _____ do not.

(4) We have two daughters; one is in Tokyo and _____ in Osaka.

(5) I don't like this red tie. Show me _____.

(6) We should be kind to_____.

(7) Can you see a big house on _____ side of the street?

(8) Three passengers were killed in the accident, but _____ were safe.

★ **2** 次の各文の（ ）内から適当なものを選べ。

(1) I've lost my camera. I have to buy a new (one，it).

(2) We don't know (neither，either) of your parents.

(3) To know is one thing; to teach is (another，the other).

(4) He doesn't care what (another，others) think of him.

(5) These apples are riper than (those，ones) in the basket.

(6) (Every，Both) of the girls play the piano.

(7) There were a lot of people on (both，each) side of the street.

(8) I'm afraid there isn't (some，any) coffee left; will you grind (some，any)?

(9) The planes took off one after (another，other).

(10) Correct errors, if (some，any), in these sentences.

3 次の各文の____に下から適当なものを選んで入れよ。ただし，同じ語を２度使わないこと。

(1) This baseball glove is too big, and that one is too small. _____ fits me.

(2) Is there any tea left in the pot?— No, there is _____.　　　　　　　　［東京経済大］

(3) Some of the passengers were injured, and _____ were killed.

(4) Don't speak ill of _____ behind their backs.

(5) He wanted to be _____, but he is now nobody.

(6) Making promises is one thing, keeping them _____.

(7) _____ of Ken's parents are on holiday now.

(8) Do you want tea or coffee?—_____. I don't mind.

〔another，both，either，somebody，neither，others，none，the others〕

advice ....

2 (3) A is one thing; B is another. 「AとBは全く別のものである。」
3 (5) nobody 「取るに足らない人物」

24 | 形容詞・副詞

🖑 要点整理

❶ 形容詞

(1) **限定用法**……名詞の前後に置き，名詞を修飾する。

> This is an **interesting** book.

> Do you have anything **interesting** to read?

(2) **叙述用法**……主格補語，目的格補語として用いられる。

> The news is very **surprising** to us.

> We painted the fence **green**.

(3) **限定用法のみ**の形容詞…… main，only，utter，mere，lone など。

叙述用法のみの形容詞…… alive，asleep，afraid，well など。

(4) **the ＋形容詞**…… the rich ＝ rich people，the old ＝ old people

(5) **数量形容詞**

数……(a) few，many，a large number of ～

量……(a) little，much，a great deal〔amount〕of ～

数・量共に可　a lot of ～（＝ lots of ～），plenty of ～

check 1 次の各文の適当な位置に，（　）内の語を入れよ。

(1) The noise kept me all night. (awake)

_____

(2) I want something to drink. (cold)

_____

(3) He wasted a deal of money on gambling. (great)

_____

❷ 副詞

(1) **動詞・形容詞・副詞・句・節**または**文全体**を修飾する。

> **Fortunately** he won the first prize.〔文全体を修飾〕

(2) **紛らわしい副詞**…… late「遅く」－ lately「最近」

hard「熱心に」－ hardly「ほとんど～ない」

(3) **注意すべき副詞**…… very は形容詞・副詞の**原級**を修飾。

much は**動詞**，形容詞・副詞の**比較級・最上級**を修飾。

check 2 次の各文の（　）内から適当なものを選べ。

(1) She got up (late, lately) this morning.

(2) It is (much, very) colder today than yesterday.

1 次の各文の（ ）内から適当なものを選べ。

(1) I can (hard, hardly) imagine she wasn't good at speaking English.

(2) John earned (a large number of, a great deal of) money.

(3) City Library has (very, much) more books than our school library does.

(4) This coffee tastes (bitter, bitterly).

(5) The (afraid, frightened) child started to cry.

2 次の各組の文を，下線部に注意して，日本語に直せ。

(1)
① The <u>late</u> Mr. Johnson was a great scientist.
（ ）
② Mr. Johnson was <u>late</u> for the meeting.
（ ）

(2)
① I don't know his <u>present</u> address.
（ ）
② Those who were <u>present</u> were all women.
（ ）

(3)
① It is <u>certain</u> that he will come tomorrow.
（ ）
② He will not come tomorrow for a <u>certain</u> reason.
（ ）

☆ **3** 日本語を参考に，（ ）内の語句を並べかえよ。ただし，不足する1語を加えること。

(1) かなり多くのコンピュータがその店から盗まれた。

(stolen / from / computers / quite / few / the shop / were).

_____.

(2) 父はめったに母と買い物に行かない。

(my mother / seldom / my father / with / shopping).

_____.

(3) この機械には何かおかしいところがある。

(something / machine / this / with / there / wrong).

_____.

4 次の各文の（ ）内に下から適当なものを選び，記号で答えよ。

(1) She is ( ) buy almost everything. ［国学院大］

　　ア enough rich to 　イ enough to rich

　　ウ rich enough to 　エ rich to enough

(2) You cannot be ( ) careful in driving a car. ［九州産業大］

　　ア far 　イ little 　ウ near 　エ too

(3) It was ( ) an interesting book that I sat up all night reading it.

　　ア much 　イ so 　ウ such 　エ very ［京都学園大］

51

25 | 前置詞 ①

要点整理

❶ 前置詞の基本

(1)　場所の前置詞

> I've spent the summer holidays **at** Nice **in** France.

> Show me the way **to** the British Museum.

> There is a picture **on** the wall.

> The sun has risen **above** the horizon.

> The girl sat **between** her parents.

> My house is **beside** the post office.

(2)　時の前置詞

> School begins **at** eight **in** the morning.

> I was born **on** July 4 **in** 1970.

> I'll wait here **till** eight. 「8時までずっと」

> I'll be back **by** eight. 「8時までには」

> Did anyone call on me **during** my absence?

> He will arrive there **in** an hour. 「(今から) 1 時間後に」

check 1 次の各文の(　)内から適当なものを選べ。

(1) He arrived (at，on) the airport.

(2) You must finish your homework (till，by) six o'clock.

(3) He was born (in，on) the morning of October 10.

❷ 前置詞の後置

> *What* are you looking **for**? 〔目的語が疑問詞〕

> *The old man* was laughed **at** by everybody. 〔群動詞の受動態〕

> I have *nothing* to write **with**. 〔不定詞の形容詞的用法〕

check 2 次の各文の適当な位置に，(　)内の前置詞を入れよ。

(1) At the station I was spoken by an American. (to)

_____

(2) There were no chairs for us to sit. (on)

_____

(3) This is the book that I've been looking. (for)

_____

★ **1** 次の各文の＿＿に下から適当な前置詞を選んで入れよ。

(1) My father often goes back and forth _____ Japan and the U.S.

(2) Finish your work _____ noon tomorrow.

(3) We are leaving for England _____ the morning of next Sunday.

(4) Mt. Fuji is over ten thousand feet _____ sea level.

(5) He was ill _____ a week and _____ that week he ate nothing.

(6) Few people can run a mile _____ four minutes.

(7) They reserved a cottage from Monday _____ Friday.

(8) You must wash your hands _____ each meal.

〔before，by，during，till，between，above，within，for，on〕

2 次の各文の適当な位置に，（　）内の前置詞を入れ，全文を書け。

(1) There is something funny him. (about)

＿＿＿＿＿＿＿＿＿＿＿＿＿＿＿＿＿＿＿＿＿＿＿＿＿＿＿＿

(2) John worked very hard, and long he became a rich man. (before)

＿＿＿＿＿＿＿＿＿＿＿＿＿＿＿＿＿＿＿＿＿＿＿＿＿＿＿＿

(3) Some people believe the existence of God. (in)

＿＿＿＿＿＿＿＿＿＿＿＿＿＿＿＿＿＿＿＿＿＿＿＿＿＿＿＿

(4) This writer has been in Japan 1985. (since)

＿＿＿＿＿＿＿＿＿＿＿＿＿＿＿＿＿＿＿＿＿＿＿＿＿＿＿＿

(5) Don't plant the flowers close that tree. (to)

＿＿＿＿＿＿＿＿＿＿＿＿＿＿＿＿＿＿＿＿＿＿＿＿＿＿＿＿

(6) The bus will be leaving twenty-five minutes. (in)   [清泉女子大-改]

＿＿＿＿＿＿＿＿＿＿＿＿＿＿＿＿＿＿＿＿＿＿＿＿＿＿＿＿

(7) We stopped at a pretty village the way to London. (on)

＿＿＿＿＿＿＿＿＿＿＿＿＿＿＿＿＿＿＿＿＿＿＿＿＿＿＿＿

3 日本語を参考に，（　）内の語句を並べかえよ。ただし，不足する１語を加えること。

(1) 彼にはいっしょに遊んでくれる友達が１人もいない。

(no / has / to / he / friends / play).

＿＿＿＿＿＿＿＿＿＿＿＿＿＿＿＿＿＿＿＿＿＿＿＿＿＿．

(2) 私の息子が興味を持っている科目は英語です。

(subject / is / the / my / son / interested / English / is).

＿＿＿＿＿＿＿＿＿＿＿＿＿＿＿＿＿＿＿＿＿＿＿＿＿＿．

(3) 私たちには生活費がもっと必要です。

(need / more / to / live / money / we).

＿＿＿＿＿＿＿＿＿＿＿＿＿＿＿＿＿＿＿＿＿＿＿＿＿＿．

(4) もっと仕事に集中できないのですか。   [独協大-改]

(you / more / work / can't / your / concentrate)?

＿＿＿＿＿＿＿＿＿＿＿＿＿＿＿＿＿＿＿＿＿＿＿＿＿＿？

要点整理

❶ 前置詞のその他の用法

(1) 原因・理由の前置詞

> His father scolded him **for** breaking the window.
> He died **of** lung cancer.
> He died **from** his wounds.
> You failed **through** your own laziness.
> My hands were blue **with** cold.

(2) 手段・道具の前置詞

> I usually go to school **by** bus.
> You must not write a letter **with** a pencil.

(3) 関連・関係の前置詞

> We have nothing to do **with** the case.
> What are you talking **about**?
> I have an interesting book **on** economics.

(4) 分離・除去の前置詞

> We are now **off** duty.
> Keep **off** the grass.
> You must be independent **of** your parents.

(5) 群前置詞……2語以上から成り，分割しては意味をなさない前置詞。

according to ～「～によれば」	**because of ～**「～の原因で」
by means of ～「～を用いて」	**in front of ～**「～の前に」
in spite of ～「～にもかかわらず」	**with regard to ～**「～に関して」
thanks to ～「～のおかげで」	**in addition to ～**「～に加えて」

check 1 次の各文の＿＿に適当な前置詞を入れよ。

(1) ＿＿＿＿＿＿ our surprise, she has gone to Africa by herself.

(2) On my way home I was caught ＿＿＿＿＿＿ a shower.

(3) Let's have a talk ＿＿＿＿＿＿ a cup of tea.

(4) The professor gave a lecture ＿＿＿＿＿＿ languages in India.

(5) They went camping ＿＿＿＿＿＿ spite of the bad weather.

(6) Thanks ＿＿＿＿＿＿ your help, I was able to succeed in business.

★ **1** 次の各文の（　）内から適当なものを選べ。

(1) He is suffering (from，of) mental illness.

(2) A large number of children are dying (with，of) hunger in the world.

(3) I'm satisfied (to，with) the result of the test.

(4) People in Europe often cut fish (by，with) scissors.

(5) We can go to the Ogasawara Islands only (by，with) ship.

(6) I'm sure Jack has something to do (with，on) that matter.

(7) My father was (on，off) duty at that time, so he couldn't go to the concert.

(8) I was robbed (by，of) my bike yesterday evening.

(9) We make soy beans (into，from) *miso*.

(10) Don't speak (in，with) your mouth full.

2 次の各文の＿＿＿に下から適当なものを選んで入れよ。

(1) ＿＿＿＿＿＿ of his selfishness he has few friends.

(2) ＿＿＿＿＿＿ to a good teacher, John passed the examination.

(3) He returned from Europe by ＿＿＿＿＿＿ of the U.S.A.

(4) ＿＿＿＿＿＿ to the weatherman, it will rain tomorrow.

(5) I'd like to stay home ＿＿＿＿＿＿ of going swimming.

〔instead，because，thanks，way，according〕

3 次の各文の（　）内に下から適当なものを選び，記号で答えよ。

(1) Kenta's parents were getting more and more angry (　　　　) him.　　　　［中部大］

　　ア on　　イ to　　ウ with　　エ against

(2) It was so nice (　　　　) you to send me a bunch of flowers.

　　ア to　　イ of　　ウ by　　エ about

(3) Bring a bottle of water just (　　　　) case you get thirsty.

　　ア in　　イ on　　ウ of　　エ at

(4) We had a very nice conversation (　　　　) lunch.　　　　［以上，神奈川大］

　　ア than　　イ over　　ウ while　　エ when

(5) The performance was far (　　　　) being perfect.　　　　［大阪経済大］

　　ア of　　イ on　　ウ to　　エ from

(6) Can you see a young woman (　　　　) white over there?　　　　［学習院大-改］

　　ア by　　イ in　　ウ on　　エ with

advice ··

2(1) selfishness「自分本位，利己主義」

装丁デザイン　ブックデザイン研究所
本文デザイン　A.S.T DESIGN
編集協力　　　群企画

大学入試 ステップアップ 英文法【基礎】

編著者	大学入試問題研究会	発行所	受験研究社
発行者	岡　本　泰　治		
印刷所	ユ　ニ　ッ　ク　ス		ⓒ 株式会社 増進堂・受験研究社

〒550-0013 大阪市西区新町2丁目19番15号
注文・不良品などについて：(06)6532-1581(代表)／本の内容について：(06)6532-1586(編集)

注意 本書を無断で複写・複製（電子化を含む）
　　 して使用すると著作権法違反となります。

Printed in Japan　高廣製本
落丁・乱丁本はお取り替えします。

大学入試 ステップ アップ

STEP UP 〆

Basic 基礎 英文法

解答・解説

解答・解説

01 基本文型　　　　　　　(pp. 4〜5)

check 1 (1) S, V, O　(2) S, V, O, C
(3) S, V, C　(4) S, V, M
(5) S, V, (I)O, (D)O

解説
(1)「客は壁に掛かっている絵をほめた。」
(2)「彼の悪い行いが、彼の父を怒らせた。」
(3)「彼は 10 年前の彼ではない。」
(4)「このペンはとてもよく書ける。」very well は write を修飾する語句で、補語ではないことに注意。
(5)「その機械は、君の手間をずいぶんと省いてくれる。」

1 (1) C　(2) O　(3) O　(4) C

解説
(1)「私は、大人になったら看護師になるつもりだ。」
(2)「私にこのカメラの使い方を教えてくれますか。」
(3)「彼女は英国から私たちに絵はがきを送ってくれた。」
(4)「私たちの新しい先生は優しそうに思える。」

2 (1) 4　(2) 1　(3) 2　(4) 5　(5) 3

解説
(1)「このシャツは(私に)4,000 円かかった。」S + V + IO + DO の文。
(2)「あなたが探している劇場は銀行の前にある。」S + V の文。in front of the bank は修飾語句。
(3)「あなたの机は頑丈に感じる。」S + V + C の文。
(4)「私は彼が無実だと信じている。」S + V + O + C の文。
(5)「私たちの先生は私たちに別のプランを提案した。」S + V + O の文。to us は修飾語句。

3 (1) He showed his album to us.
(2) He bought a fur coat for his wife.
(3) The teacher told a mysterious story to us yesterday.

解説
〈S + V + IO + DO〉の語順を変えて、〈S + V + DO +前置詞＋人〉にすることができる。

前置詞 to を使う動詞… give, hand, lend, pay, tell, send など。for を使う動詞… buy, cook, find, make など。of を使う動詞… ask

4 (1)①「彼女はその知らせを聞いて青くなった。」
②「彼女はその角で左に曲がった。」
(2)①「私の父は健康を保つため、毎朝走る。」
②「私の父は市の中心部で中華料理店を経営している。」
(3)①「彼は息子に莫大な財産を残した。」
②「彼は息子を一人にしておいた。」
(4)①「私は容易にその英語の本を見つけた。」
②「私はその英語の本が易しいとわかった。」

02 基本時制　　　　　　　(pp. 6〜7)

check 1 (1) rains　(2) will rain
(3) goes　(4) studied　(5) arrives
(6) had　(7) travels

解説
(1)「もし明日雨が降れば、出発を延期しよう。」この場合の if 節は副詞節なので、内容が未来でも現在形を用いる。
(2)「明日は雨が降るのだろうか。」この場合の if 節は名詞節なので未来形を用いる。
(3)「近ごろ、彼女は日曜日に買い物に出かける。」現在の習慣。
(4)「アメリカにいたときに、彼は英語を勉強した。」
(5)「私たちが待っている飛行機はもうすぐ到着する。」発着の予定を表す現在形。
(6)「私は彼が携帯電話を持っていると思ったが、持っていなかった。」時制の一致。
(7)「私たちは、光より速く進むものはないと学んだ。」that 節の内容は「真理」なので、時制の一致を受けない。

check 2 (1)「私は英国で夏の休暇を過ごすつもりだ。」
(2)「外出してはいけません。もうすぐ昼食です。」

解説

(1) be going to 〜は近接未来とも呼ばれ，「〜するつもりである，〜しようとするところだ」などの意味に用いる。

(2) be about to 〜は，be going to 〜よりも「まさに〜しようとしている」の意味が明確に表される。

---

1 (1) will succeed (2) is (3) changes
(4) bought (5) smokes (6) saw

解説

(1)「来年，彼は試験に合格するだろうか。」この if 節は名詞節なので未来形を用いる。

(2) that 節の内容は「真理」なので，時制の一致を受けない。

(3) until 節は副詞節なので，未来形の代わりに現在形を用いる。

(4) two years ago「2年前」

(5)「私の父は食事のときには決してたばこを吸わない。」現在の習慣。

(6) last「最後に」過去を表す副詞。

---

2 (1) is about to rain (2) would
(3) will go (4) took (5) is

解説

(1)「急ぐべきだ」とあるので今まさに雨が降ろうとしている。

(2)時制の一致。

(3)「暖かい空気は上るものだ。」will には「習性」を表す用法もある。

(4) in those days「当時」とあるので，過去の習慣。

(5)未来形の代わりに現在形を用いる。

---

3 (1) F (2) T (3) F (4) T
(5) T (6) F (7) T

解説

(1) before 以下は現在形を用いる。

(2) that 以下は「真理」。

(3) is going to は未来を表す。

(4)過去の習慣を表す文。

(5)この when 節は名詞節。

(6)疑問詞 when と現在完了をいっしょに用いることはできない。

(7)「油は水に浮くものだ。」習性を表す。

---

4 (1) are, going, to (2) he, was

解説

(1) will と be going to 〜

(2)直接話法から間接話法への書き換え。that 節内の人称と時制の変化に注意。

03 完了形・進行形　　　(pp. 8〜9)

check 1 (1) have lost (2) had lived
(3) had bought (4) will have finished

解説

(1)「私はかさをなくしてしまった。」

(2)「私たちは引っ越す以前，福岡に住んでいた。」継続用法の過去完了。

(3)「彼は私がその時計を買ったことを知らなかった。」私が「買った」のは彼が「知らなかった」時点よりさらに前。過去完了には，このように「ある過去を基準にしてそれより前の時」を表す用法(大過去)もある。

(4)「私は1時間もすれば宿題を終えているだろう。」完了用法の未来完了。

---

check 2 (1) has been writing (2) was
knocking (3) will be raining

解説

(1)現在完了進行形は have〔has〕been 〜ing の形。

(2)過去進行形は was〔were〕〜ing の形。

(3)未来進行形は will be 〜ing の形。

---

1 (1)あなたはもう，図書館で借りた本を読みましたか。

(2)彼は昨年まで，長い間私と会っていなかった。

(3)私たちがいっしょに行ったとき以前に，あなたはロサンゼルスを訪れたことがあったのですか。

(4)私たちは来月で，結婚して30年になる。

(5)彼は起きたときからずっとテレビゲームをしている。

(6)私は明日のこの時間，スタジアムで叫んでいるだろう。

解説

(1)完了用法の現在完了。

(2)継続用法の過去完了。

(3)経験用法の過去完了。

(4)継続用法の未来完了。
(5)現在完了進行形。継続用法の現在完了と同じく，「(ずっと)〜している」と訳す。
(6)未来進行形。

2 (1)ア (2)エ (3)エ (4)ア

解説

(1) belong to 〜「〜に属する」は状態を表す動詞なので，進行形にならない。
(2)「私が聞いた」のは過去で，それより前に「5回仕事を変えていた」ため過去完了。
(3) since は現在完了(進行)形で用いられる。
(4)意味の上では未来(完了)だが，条件を表す副詞節なので，代わりに現在(完了)を用いる。

3 (1) had, met(seen), before
(2) has, been, to
(3) have, finished(done)
(4) You're, doubting

解説

(1)「彼女が言った」より前の「過去の時」なので過去完了を用いる。
(2) have〔has〕been to 〜「〜に行ってきたところだ，〜に行ったことがある」と have〔has〕gone to 〜「〜に行ってしまった(今はここにいない)」を混同しないこと。
(3)条件・時を表す副詞節では，未来(完了)形の代わりに，現在(完了)形を用いる。
(4)非難を表す現在進行形。

04 助動詞 ① (pp. 10〜11)

check 1 (1) Would (2) would
(3) should (4) can't (5) won't
(6) should

解説

(1) would like (to) 〜「〜がほしいのですが，〜をしたいのですが」は控えめな表現。Would you like 〜?「〜はいかがですか」と人にものを勧める表現としても用いる。
(2)過去の習慣を表している。「よく〜したものだ」
(3)義務・当然(〜すべきである)を表している。
(4) can は否定形で「〜のはずがない」と，強い否定的推量を表す。反対は，He must be ill.(彼は病気に違いない。)

(5)主語の固執・拒絶を表す。「この箱はどうしても閉まらない。」
(6)感情の原因・判断・命令・提案の内容を表す that 節内では，〈should +動詞の原形〉を用いる。米用法では should を省略し，主語や時制にかかわらず動詞の原形を使うことが多い。
e.g. It is surprising that she (should) say such a rude thing.

1 (1) would (2) should
(3) can't(cannot) (4) been (5) won't

解説

(1)過去の習慣を表す would「よく〜したものだ」。
(2)感情の原因を表す that 節内では，should(英用法)を用いる。
(3)強い否定的推量「〜のはずがない」を表す can't。
(4)現在完了 +〈be able to 〜〉なので，been を用いる。
(5)主語の強い拒絶の意志「どうしても〜しない」の won't。

2 (1) could (2) Shall (3) Shall
(4) can (5) should

解説

(1)「〜することができた」
(2)「私に〜してほしいですか」→「(私が)〜しましょうか」
(3)「(いっしょに)〜しましょうか」
(4)「〜のしかたを知っている」→「〜できる」
(5)「医者は私に，毎朝散歩するよう助言した。」要求・必要・提案を表す that 節内では，〈(should +)動詞の原形〉が用いられる。

3 (1)①タカシはシンガポールに住んでいたので，英語と中国語を話すことができる。
②タカシは今，シンガポールにいるので，ここにいるはずはない。
(2)①私たちはバスに乗るべきだ。あまり時間がない。②バスに乗ったら，1時間ぐらいかかるはずだ。
(3)①水をいただきたいのですが。
②いやな臭いがしたので，少年はどうしてもその牛乳を飲もうとしなかった。

解説

(1)①能力を表す。②否定的推量を表す。
(2)①当然・必要を表す。②当然の推量を表す。

(3)① 丁寧な表現。〈would like to ＋動詞の原形〉「〜したいのですが」② will〔would〕には固執・拒絶を表す，「どうしても〜しようとする〔した〕」という用法もある。

05 助動詞 ②　　　　　　　　　(pp. 12〜13)

check 1　(1) May　(2) must　(3) need

解説
(1)「私はもう帰ってもいいですか。」「いいえ，いけません。」
Must I leave now? の場合は答え方が異なる。
－ Yes, you *must.*
－ No, { you *need not.*
{ you *don't have to.*
(〜する必要はない)
(2) must「〜に違いない」は強い肯定的推量を表す。
(3) need not 〜「〜する必要はない」(助動詞用法) ＝ don't need to 〜(動詞用法)

check 2　(1) used　(2) ought

解説
(1) used to 〜「よく〜したものだ，かつては〜であった」は過去の習慣・状態を表す。
(2) ought to 〜 ＝ should 〜「〜するべきである，〜のはずだ」should と同様に義務・当然を表す。

[発展]
(1)彼はなぜここにいないのですか。彼は列車に乗り遅れたに違いない。
(2)ケイトは電話に出なかった。彼女は眠っていたのかもしれない。
(3)ジョンがこの本を読んだはずがない。それは難しすぎる。
(4)君は入ってくる前にノックをすべきだったのに。

1　(1)このレストランではたばこを吸ってはいけません。
(2)この本を１週間で読み終えるのは難しいに違いない。
(3)よくもこんな夜遅く来られるものだ。
(4)あなたはこんな晴れた日に部屋にいるべきではない。
(5)私はよく部員とバレーボールをしたものだ。

解説
(1) must の否定文は禁止を表す。
(2)この must は強い推量を表す。
(3) How dare you 〜? は慣用表現で，「よくも〜できるものだ」の意味。他人に対する憤慨を表す。
(4) ought to は should と同じく義務・当然を表し，否定形は ought not to となる。
(5) used to は過去の習慣を表す。

2　(1) May　(2) ought　(3) needn't
(4) can't〔cannot〕

解説
(1)「〜を願っています」→「〜 しますように」may には祈願の意味があり，その場合は〈May ＋主語＋動詞〜!〉の語順。
(2)「私たちはすぐホテルに戻るべきだと思う。」should, ought to ともに義務・当然を表す。
(3)「〜する必要はない」を助動詞 need の否定短縮形で表す。
(4)「ジュディは不注意であるに違いない」→「ジュディは注意深いはずがない」must「〜に違いない」の対義語は can't〔cannot〕「〜のはずがない」なので注意。

3　(1) ought, have, arrived
(2) needn't, have, woken〔woke, waked〕
(3) must, have, gone
(4) may, have, missed
(5) can't〔cannot〕, have, done

解説
〈助動詞 ＋ have ＋過去分詞〉のいろいろ。
(1) should〔ought to〕＋ have ＋過去分詞「当然〜しているはずだ，〜すべきであったのに」
(2) need not ＋ have ＋過去分詞「〜する必要はなかったのに」
(3) must ＋ have ＋過去分詞「〜したに違いない」
(4) may ＋ have ＋過去分詞「〜したかもしれない」
(5) can't〔cannot〕＋ have ＋過去分詞「〜だったはずがない」

06 不定詞①　　(pp. 14〜15)

check 1 (1)名詞的用法　(2)副詞的用法
(3)形容詞的用法

解説
(1)「私たちのできることは,警察を呼ぶことだけだ。」
(2)「私はあなたの結婚について聞いてうれしい。」
(3)「昼食に食べるものが何かありますか。」

check 2 (1) The doctor advised <u>me</u> to give up drinking.
(2) It is impossible <u>for you</u> to read a hundred pages in an hour.
(3) It is very careless <u>of him</u> to do such a thing!

解説
(1)〈advise + 人 + to 〜〉「(人)に〜するように忠告する」
(2)通例, 不定詞の意味上の主語は不定詞の直前に置き,〈for + 人 + to 〜〉とする。
(3)〈It is + 人の性質を表す形容詞 + of + 人 + to 〜〉人の性質を表す形容詞 kind, nice, stupid, wise などの場合,〈of + 人〉で不定詞の意味上の主語を表す。

check 3 (1) to, have, been
(2) to, have, been
(3) reported, to, have

解説
不定詞の時制が述語動詞より前のときは, 完了不定詞にする。

1 (1) It　(2) of　(3) to　(4) how　(5) for

解説
(1) to swim 以下を表す形式主語。
(2) silly「まぬけな」は人の性質を表す形容詞。
(3) It is believed that she is over ninety. と書き換えることができる。
(4)〈疑問詞 + to 〜〉cf. when to start「いつ出発すべきか」, what to say「何を言うべきか」, how to drive「いかに運転すべきか」
(5)「毎朝, 運動するのは私たちにとって良いことだ。」〈for + 人〉で不定詞の意味上の主語を表す。

2 (1) to live in　(2) what to do next
(3) everybody's duty to obey the law
(4) very kind of you to help me
(5) to have got(gotten) lost in the fog

解説
(1)「私たちには住む家がない。」形容詞的用法。
(2)「次に何をすべきか彼女にはわからなかった。」〈疑問詞 + to 〜〉
(3)「法に従うのは皆の義務だ。」
(4)「私を助けてくれるなんて, あなたはとても親切ですね。」
(5)「彼らは霧の中で道に迷ってしまったようだ。」

3 (1) to have kept you waiting
(2) told her grandchildren not to go out
(3) you like me to make strong tea for
(4) you have to do is follow

解説
(1)〈to have + 過去分詞〉は完了不定詞で, 述語動詞の時制より前の時を表す。この場合, 省略されている I'm(sorry)より前ということ。
(2)不定詞の否定は〈not + to 〜〉。
(3) would like + 人 + to 〜「(人)に〜してほしい」
(4)この場合,(to)follow の to は省略されている。

07 不定詞②　　(pp. 16〜17)

check 1 (1) speak　(2) not follow　(3) cry
(4) work　(5) to accept

解説
(1)〈感覚動詞 + 人 + 原形不定詞〉「あなたは彼が人の悪口を言うのを今までに聞いたことがありますか。」
(2)〈had better (not) + 原形不定詞〉「〜する〔しない〕ほうがよい」
(3)〈cannot (help) but + 原形不定詞〉「〜せざるを得ない」= cannot help 〜ing
(4)〈make + 人 + 原形不定詞〉「(人)に〜させる」
(5)使役動詞のうちで,〈get + 人 + to 〜〉「(人)に〜させる」のように to 不定詞をとるのは get だけである。

check 2 (1) too, to　(2) order, to
(3) so, as

(1)「その女性はあまりに速く話したので，私は彼女の言うことが理解できなかった。」

(2)「私は学校に間に合うように早く起きた。」so as to ～ = in order to ～

(3)「彼女は親切にも私に道を教えてくれた。」so ... as to ～「～するほど…だ」目的を表す so as to ～ と混同しないこと。

1 (1) too, for　(2) enough, to
(3) so, as(in, order)　(4) so, as
(5) afford, to　(6) better, go
(7) fails, to

解説

(1)「この問題は難しすぎて私には解けない。」この beyond は「～の能力をこえて」。

(2) ... enough to ～「～するのに十分…だ」

(3) 目的を表す so as to ～ = in order to ～「～するために」

(4) so ... as to ～「～するほど…だ」「彼女は私に金を貸してくれるほど親切だった。」

(5) cannot afford to ～「～する余裕がない」

(6) 〈had better + 原形〉「～ したほうがよい」

(7) never fail to ～「必ず～する」

2 (1) cross　(2) to shake　(3) wash
(4) better not　(5) to fix

解説

(1) 〈感覚動詞 + 人 + 原形不定詞〉

(2) They felt the floor shake. の受動態を考える。受動態では原形不定詞に to がつく。

(3) 〈have + 人 + 原形不定詞〉「(人)に～させる，(人)に～してもらう」

(4) 〈had better + 原形不定詞〉の否定は，〈had better + not + 原形不定詞〉「～ しないほうがよい」。

(5) 〈get + 人 + to ～〉「(人)に～させる，(人)に～ してもらう」

3 (1)エ　(2)カ　(3)ウ　(4)イ　(5)ア　(6)オ

解説

(1) to make matters worse「さらに悪いことに」

(2) to begin with「まず第一に」

(3) to tell the truth「実を言うと」

(4) to be sure「確かに」

(5) to say nothing of ～「～は言うまでもなく」

(6) so to speak「いわば」

08 動名詞 ①　　(pp. 18～19)

check 1　(1)①　(2)①　(3)②　(4)②　(5)①

解説

(1)「散歩することは私たちの健康に良い。」文の主語で名詞の役割をしている。

(2)「交通の激しい通りを渡るときは，気をつけなさい。」前置詞の後ろに(準)動詞を置くときは動名詞を用いる。

(3)「散歩している」と訳せるので現在分詞。

(4) 現在分詞の後置修飾。「ベッドで寝ている赤ちゃん」

(5)「たばこを吸うための部屋〔喫煙室〕」用途を表す動名詞。

check 2　(1)①彼は有名な医者であることを誇りにしている。②彼は父親が有名な医者であることを誇りにしている。
(2)①私は試験に合格すると確信している。②私は彼が試験に合格すると確信している。

check 3　(1) having, broken
(2) not, having

解説

(1) 主節と that 節内の「時」のずれは，完了形動名詞で表す。「私は約束を破ってしまったことをすまなく思っている。」

(2) not は動名詞の直前に置く。「私は若いときに一生懸命勉強しなかったことを後悔している。」

1 (1)イ　(2)ア　(3)ウ　(4)ウ　(5)ア

解説

(1)「レポートを速く書くことはうまく書くことほど重要ではない。」

(2)「私たちはリサイクルすることによって，環境を保護することができる。」by ～ing「～することによって」

(3) not を動名詞の直前に置く。「あなたに事実を話さず，申し訳ない。」

(4)「私はあなたが彼に車を貸すのが気に入らない。」動名詞の意味上の主語は，所有格または目的格を直前に置いて表す。

(5) Would you mind my ～ing?「私が～することをいやがりますか。」→「(私が)～してもかまいませんか。」mind は「いやがる」なので，否定の答えが了承を表す。

2 (1) Swimming　(2) having, stolen
　　(3) on, my, respecting　(4) without
　　(5) of, his, becoming

解説
(1)「暑い日に泳ぐことはとても楽しい。」
(2)「彼は金を盗んだことを否定した。」
(3)「彼は私が両親を敬うべきだと主張した。」
(4) without 〜ing「〜せずに」
(5)「彼が会長になる望みはありますか。」類似の構文
　　として，There is no possibility of his becoming
　　president.（彼が会長になる可能性はない。）

3 (1) of, making, speaking
　　(2) of(about), having, been
　　(3) not, having

解説
(1) be afraid of 〜ing「〜することを恐れる」, in 〜
　　ing「〜するときに」
(2) He complained that he had been treated unfairly.
　　から考える。
(3) 否定語は動名詞の前に置く。

09 動名詞 ②　　　　　　　　　(pp. 20〜21)

check 1　(1) opening　(2) watching
　　(3) playing　(4) watching

解説
(1) mind 〜ing「〜することをいやがる」の意味から,
　　Would you mind opening the window?「窓を開けて
　　くれますか。」の意味となる。
(2) stop 〜ing「〜するのをやめる」, stop to 〜「〜す
　　るために立ち止まる」の違いに注意。
(3) practice 〜ing「〜の練習をする」
(4) enjoy 〜ing「〜することを楽しむ」

check 2　①この本を一度読んだことを覚え
　　ている。
　　②この本を読むことを覚えていてください。

解説
forget 〜ing「〜したことを忘れる」, forget to 〜「〜
するのを忘れる」：try 〜ing「〜してみる」, try to 〜
「〜しようと努める」などの意味の違いに注意。

check 3　(1) On, arriving

(2) no, accounting
(3) prevented(kept), from

解説
(1) on 〜ing「〜するとすぐに」
(2)「人の趣味を説明することはできない。」〔たで食う
　　虫も好き好き。〕（ことわざ）「There is no 〜ing.「〜
　　することは不可能だ。」
(3) prevent〔keep〕+ O + from 〜ing「O が〜するのを
　　妨げる」

1 (1) keeping　(2) seeing
　　(3) keeping　(4) laughing　(5) to mail

解説
(1) avoid 〜ing「〜することを避ける」
(2) look forward to 〜ing「〜することを楽しみにして
　　いる」
(3) get〔be〕used to 〜ing「〜することに慣れる〔慣れ
　　ている〕」
(4) cannot help 〜ing「〜せざるを得ない」
(5)「明日，この手紙を出すのを忘れないようにしな
　　さい。」forget 〜ing「〜したことを忘れる」は不適
　　当。

2 (1)ウ　(2)イ　(3)ウ　(4)エ　(5)ウ　(6)ア
　　(7)イ

解説
(1) Would you mind 〜ing?「〜していただけますか。」
　　Would you mind my 〜ing?「（私が）〜してもかま
　　いませんか。」と区別する。
(2) decide は不定詞のみを目的語にとる。
(3) It goes without saying that 〜.「〜 は言うまでもな
　　い。」
(4)「彼はピアノを弾こうとしたが，できなかった。」
　　try 〜ing「〜 してみる」では意味が通らない。
(5)「彼は健康の問題により，たばこをやめなければ
　　ならなかった。」give up は動名詞のみを目的語に
　　とる。
(6) There is no 〜ing.「〜するのは不可能だ。」
(7)「私は子どものとき，兄〔弟〕と公園で遊んだのを
　　覚えている。」remember to 〜「〜するのを覚えて
　　おく」は不適当。

3 (1) at, painting　(2) from, attending
　　(3) worth, visiting　(4) to, eating
　　(5) like, watching
　　(6) without, thinking

(1) be good at ～ing「～するのが得意だ」

(2) keep〔prevent〕＋人＋from ～ing「(人)が～することを妨げる」

(3) be worth ～ing「～する価値がある」

(4) be used to ～ing「～することに慣れている」

(5) feel like ～ing「したい気がする」

(6) never ... without ～ing「…すれば必ず～する」

10 分 詞 ①　(pp. 22～23)

check 1　(1) Barking　(2) injured
(3) sitting　(4) nodding　(5) written
(6) understood

解説

1. 現在分詞「～している」……能動的意味を持つ。
   a *sleeping baby*「眠っている赤ん坊」= a baby who is sleeping
2. 過去分詞
   ① 自動詞の過去分詞「～してしまっている」……完了の意味を持つ。*fallen* leaves「落ちてしまっている葉→落ち葉」= leaves which have fallen
   ② 他動詞の過去分詞「～された」……受動的意味を持つ。an *injured* boy「けがをさせられた少年→ けがをした少年」= a boy who was injured

check 2　(1) had my bicycle repaired
(2) had my bag stolen

解説

「～ してもらった」、「～された」の違いは文脈による。

1　(1) People living in the city like to visit the country.
(2) He bought a book written in English yesterday.
(3) My brother left the water running.
(4) The injured people were all taken to the nearest hospital.
(5) The number of people injured in the traffic accident has not been known.

解説

(1)「都市に住んでいる人々」
(2)「英語で書かれている本」
(3)「水を流れているままにしておいた」
(4)「けがをした人々」
(5)「交通事故でけがをした人々」

2　(1) broken　(2) interesting
(3) increasing　(4) fallen　(5) surprising
(6) called　(7) lying　(8) surprised

解説

(1)「壊れたイス」
(2)「おもしろいように思えた」
(3)「増大する人口」
(4)「落ちてしまった葉〔落ち葉〕」
(5)「驚くべき知らせ」
(6)「あなたの名前が呼ばれるのを」
(7)「床に横たわっている老人」
(8)「驚いたように見えた」

3　(1) used　(2) living　(3) painted, by
(4) have, waiting　(5) closed

解説

(1)「だれかが以前に所有した」→「中古の」
(2)「空室だ」→「住んでいる人がいない」
(3) wall は paint「塗る」の動作を受ける側なので，過去分詞を用いる。
(4) to have kept は完了不定詞。keep + O + waiting「O を待たせておく」
(5)〈with ＋物＋過去分詞〉「(物)がされている〔された〕まま」

4　(1) running　(2) heard
(3) drowning　(4) stamped　(5) cut

解説

(1)「小犬が走りながら私を追いかけてきた。」
(2)「部屋が騒々しいので，私は自分の言うことを聞いてもらえなかった。」
(3)「おぼれる者はわらをもつかむ。」(ことわざ)
(4)「メアリーは入国管理所でパスポートにスタンプを押してもらった。」
(5)「髪が長すぎるので，切ってもらいたい。」

11 分 詞 ②　　　(pp. 24〜25)

check 1　(1) Coming, home
　(2) Having, nothing

解説

主節と従属節の主語と時制がともに同一の例である。

check 2　(1) Having, finished
　(2) Not, having, seen

解説

(1)従属節の時制は主節のそれより前であるので，〈Having ＋過去分詞〉となる。
(2)分詞の否定は，否定語をその直前に置く。

check 3　(1) It being very cold, we stayed indoors all day.
　(2) There being no bus service, we had to walk home.

解説

分詞と述語動詞の主語が同一ではないので両方の主語が必要になる。
(1)「とても寒かったので，1日中家の中にいた。」
(2)「バスの便がなかったので，家へ歩いて帰らなければならなかった。」

1　(1) Having locked the door, I went to bed.
　(2) The summer holidays being over, we came back to school.
　(3) It being fine tomorrow, we will go fishing.
　(4) Seen from a distance, the mountain looks like a lion.

解説

(1)従属節の時制が主節の時制より前であるので，〈Having ＋過去分詞〉とする。
(2), (3)従属節の主語が主節の主語と同一ではないので，両方ともに主語が必要。
(4)従属節が受動態の場合は〈Being ＋過去分詞〜〉の Being はよく省略される。

2　(1)エ　(2)ウ　(3)エ　(4)イ　(5)ア

解説

(1)「カフェテリアに入ると，友人の1人が昼食を食べているのが見えた。」
(2)「十分なお金がなかったので，彼女は新車を買うのは難しいと気づいた。」
(3)「コンピュータの電源を入れて，彼はEメールをチェックした。」
(4)「電車の便がなかったので，そこへ行く別の方法を見つけなければならなかった。」As there was 〜 が分詞構文になった形。
(5)「年齢を考慮すると，彼は若く見える。」

3　(1) Never having (Having never) read the book
　(2) While staying in London
　(3) Judging from his appearance

解説

(1)「その本を一度も読んだことがないので，批評することはできない。」
(2)「ロンドンに滞在中に，私はこれらのコインを収集した。」分詞構文の意味をはっきりさせたいときは，while などの接続詞を置くことがある。
(3)慣用的独立分詞構文。judging from 〜「〜から判断すると」，strictly speaking「厳密に言うと」，generally speaking「一般的に言うと」

12 受け身 ①　　　(pp. 26〜27)

check 1　(1) The car was washed by Mike yesterday.
　(2) I was given a dictionary by my uncle on my birthday. (A dictionary was given (to) me by my uncle on my birthday.)
　(3) The baby was named John by the (his) parents.

解説

(2)目的語が2つあるので，受動態も2種類。

check 2　(1) in　(2) with
　(3) with (at, by)

解説

(1) be interested in 〜「〜に興味がある」
(2) be covered with 〜「〜に覆われている」
(3) be delighted with (at, by) 〜「〜に喜ぶ」

1 (1) from (2) after (3) in

解説
(1) *e.g.* Cheese is made from milk.「チーズは牛乳から作られる。」⇄ Milk is made into cheese.「牛乳はチーズになる。」
(2) be named after ～「～にちなんで名づけられる」
(3) be caught in「(にわか雨など)に遭う」

2 (1) was, surprised, at (by)
(2) was, satisfied, with
(3) is, known, to
(4) is, spoken, in, Mexico

解説
(1) be surprised at〔by〕～「～を聞いて〔見て〕驚く」
(2) be satisfied with ～「～に満足する」
(3) be known to ～「～に知られている」
(4) by them は「一般の人々」なので省略されている。

3 (1) The baby was saved by a fireman.
(2) The telephone was invented by Bell in 1876.
(3) The fence was painted red by my father.
(4) Eggs are not(aren't) sold at the store.
(5) The children were told an amusing story by an old man.
An amusing story was told (to) the children by an old man.

解説
(4) by them は省略する。
(5) 目的語が2つあるので，受動態も2種類。

4 (1) Mr. Smith teaches us English.
(2) They(People) speak English in Australia.
(3) Everyone calls him Honest John.
(4) The parents left the baby alone.
(5) John's teacher scolded him for being late for school.

解説
(2) もとの受動態の文には動作主が明示されていないので，They〔People〕を主語にする。

13 受け身 ② (pp. 28～29)

check 1 (1) Who was this box made by?
(2) I will be invited to the party by Lucy (invited by Lucy to the party).
(3) She was seen to sing on the stage by Tom.
(4) His words were paid no attention to (by us). (No attention was paid to his words (by us).)

解説
(1) 能動態の文の主語である Who ～? は受動態の文では，By whom ～? の形で文頭にくるか，Who ～ by?(口語)とする。By whom was this box made? は古い表現。
(2) 助動詞(will, can, must など)があれば，〈助動詞＋be ＋過去分詞〉とする。
(3) 感覚動詞や使役動詞を受動態にすると，補語の原形不定詞は to 不定詞になる。
(4) 2種類の受動態ができることに注意。*e.g.* We should take good care of the children. → ① *The children* should be taken good care of (by us). ② *Good care* should be taken of the children (by us).

1 (1) The large museum is being built in the park.
(2) The boy is often made fun of by his friends.
(3) A stranger was seen to enter my house.
(4) The meeting will be put off till next Sunday.

解説
(1)「建設されている」の意味で〈be 動詞＋ being ＋過去分詞〉の形を用いる。
(2)「からかわれている」の意味で of が必要。make fun of ～「～をからかう」
(3) 受動態では，感覚動詞を用いた文の補語は to 不定詞にする。
(4)「延期される」という受動態の意味で be が必要。

2 ⑴ He was looked down on as a liar (by them).

⑵ The student's homework has just been done by him.

⑶ Dinner is being cooked by Mother in the kitchen.

⑷ When will the meeting be held by the committee?

⑸ The children's mother was being watched to make a doll by them.

解説

⑴ look down on ～「～を軽べつする」は群動詞なので，切りはなさない。

⑵現在完了の受動態〈have〔has〕been ＋過去分詞〉となる。

⑶進行形の受動態〈be 動詞＋ being ＋過去分詞〉となる。

⑷〈助動詞＋ be ＋過去分詞〉とする。

⑸感覚動詞 watch を受動態にすると，補語の原形不定詞 make は to make となる。

3 ⑴① It, is, said ② is, said, to

⑵ heard, to, complain ⑶① must, be, taken ② must, be, taken

解説

⑴ It is said that ～. の It は that 節の内容を表す形式主語である。この書き換えはよく出題される。

⑵感覚動詞の受動態なので，complain → to complain とする。

⑶ **check 3** ⑷の **解説** を参照。

4 ⑴ spoken(talked), to ⑵ be, eaten

⑶ made, to ⑷ laughed, at

解説

⑴群動詞 speak to ～「～に話しかける」の受動態。

⑵「この魚」は食べられる側なので受動態にする。〈助動詞＋ be ＋過去分詞〉の形。

⑶使役の表現〈make ＋人＋原形不定詞〉「(人)に～させる」の受動態。使役動詞を受動態にすると，原形不定詞が to 不定詞になる。

⑷群動詞 laugh at ～「～を笑う」の受動態。

14 比 較 ①

check 1 ⑴ bigger ⑵ better
⑶ largest ⑷(the) most fluently
⑸ exciting

解説

⑵ well − better − best の不規則変化。

⑷形容詞に -ly をつけた副詞は，carefully − more carefully − most carefully のように，前に more, most をつける。

check 2 ⑴① valuable, as
② Time, more ③ the, most
⑵① the, highest ② higher, any
③ No ④ No, higher

解説

よく出題される書き換え問題である。同じ意味を最上級，比較級，原級で表現できることに注意。

1 ⑴ more diligent, most diligent

⑵ happier, happiest

⑶ more carefully, most carefully

⑷ thinner, thinnest

⑸ more slowly, most slowly

⑹ less, least ⑺ fewer, fewest

⑻ more, most ⑼ more, most

⑽ worse, worst

⑾ worse, worst ⑿ better, best

⒀ better, best

⒁ farther, farthest
(further, furthest)

⒂ later, latest (latter, last)

解説

⑸〈形容詞＋ ly〉は 2 音節でも more ～, most ～ とする。

⒁ far − farther − farthest は距離に，far − further − furthest は程度・時間などに用いるとされるが，further − furthest を距離にも用いる傾向がある。

⒂ late − later − latest は時間に，late − latter − last は順序に用いられる。

2 ⑴ better ⑵ more important
⑶ cheapest ⑷ latter ⑸ later

(2)「自分自身を知ることは，他のどんなことより重要だ。」

(4)「この本の後半部」の意味。

(5)「太陽は冬より夏に遅く沈む。」の意味。時間の差を表す比較級は later。

3 (1) more, pleasant　(2) more, any
(3) No, longer
(4) most, interesting, ever

解説

(1)原級の表現を比較級で書き換える。「旅より楽しいものはない。」

(2)最上級の表現を比較級で書き換える。「金は他のどんな金属より価値がある。」〈any other + 単数名詞〉に注意。

(3)最上級の表現を否定の主語を用いた比較級で書き換える。「アメリカのどんな川もミシシッピ川より長くはない。」

(4)否定を用いた表現を，最上級で書き換える。「これは私が今までに聞いた中で最もおもしろい話だ。」

4 (1) It is <u>much</u> colder today than yesterday.
(2) He looks <u>worse</u> than yesterday.
(3) Ted is the smartest boy <u>in</u> our class.
(4) Bob is the <u>taller</u> of the twin brothers.

解説

(1)比較級の強調は much。

(2) ill － worse － worst

(3)〈in + 比較の対象が属する範囲，社会，団体など〉で class, city, world などの単数名詞，〈of + 具体的に比較の対象となるもの〉で them all, the five などの複数名詞。

(4)〈the + 比較級 + of + 2つ〔2人〕〉「2つ〔2人〕のうちで～なほう」

5 (1) the most wonderful apple I have ever
(2) producing more cars than any other country
(3) makes her look much younger than she really is

解説

(1) I have never tasted such a wonderful apple as this. と書き換え可。

(2) No other country is now producing more cars than this country. と書き換え可。

15 比　較 ②　　　(pp. 32～33)

check **1** (1) soon, as
(2) times, large, as
(3) not, so, much

解説

(1)〈as + 形容詞〔副詞〕+ as + S + can〉「S ができるだけ～」

(2) ... times as ～ as「…倍だけ～である」の形式で倍数を表す。*e.g.* This box is *twice*〔*three times*〕 *as* large *as* that.「この箱はあの箱の2倍〔3倍〕の大きさだ。」

(3) not so much A as B「A というよりむしろ B」

check **2** (1) The, higher, the, colder
(2) at, least

解説

(1)〈the + 比較級～，the + 比較級 ...〉「～すればするほど，ますます…だ」

(2) not less than = at least「少なくとも」

check **3** (1) highest　(2) best　(3) least

解説

(1)「K 2 は世界で 2 番目に高い山である。」

(2)「梅の花は，2，3日すれば満開だろう。」

(3) at least「少なくとも」

1 (1)石狩川は日本で3番目に長い川だ。
(2)その選手は昨日の試合で絶好調だった。
(3)私の部屋は姉（妹）の部屋の半分の広さだ。
(4)そのテストの問題はだんだん難しくなっていた。
(5)私のスーツケースは少なくとも 15kg の重さがある。
(6)彼女はボーイフレンドより3歳年下だ。
(7)これは私が今まで食べた中で最もおいしいステーキだ。
(8)若ければ若いほど，何かに慣れるのは簡

単だ。

(9)彼はピアニストというよりむしろ作曲家だ。

(10)私がこのレポートを書き終えるのにかかるのは，せいぜい２時間だろう。

解説

(3)倍数は〈X times as 〜 as ...〉で表す。X times 以外には，twice「２倍」，half「半分」，a quarter「４分の１」などがある。

(4)〈比較級 and 比較級〉は「だんだん〜，ますます〜」の意味。more を使う比較級ならば，more だけを重ねる。

(6)差を表す場合，by 〜を文末に置くか，by なしで比較級の直前に置く。

(7)〈the ＋最上級（＋ that）＋ S ＋ have ever ＋過去分詞〉「今までに〜した中で最も…」

(10) not more than ＝ at most「多くても，せいぜい」 no more than「しか」と区別すること。

2 (1) prefer, playing (2) higher, mountain (3) he, could (4) no, more

解説

(1)「私は野球をするより見るほうが好きだ。」prefer A to B「BよりAが好きだ」この to は不定詞の to ではなく前置詞なので，あとは動名詞が適切。

(2)「エベレストは世界でいちばん高い山だ。」→「エベレストは世界のほかのどの山よりも高い。」〈比較級 ＋ than　any　other ＋ 単数名詞〉「ほかのどの〜よりも…」

(3)「彼はできるだけすばやく昼食をとった。」as 〜 as S can ＝ as 〜 as possible で「できるだけ〜」。can を過去形にする点に注意。

(4)「私たちは京都に２日間しか滞在しなかった。」no more than「〜 しか」は more を使うが，少なさを強調する表現なので注意。

16 関係詞 ① (pp. 34〜35)

check 1 (1) What, what (2) that (3) who(that)

解説

(1)「君の言ったことと君のしたことは一致しなかった。」

(2)「君のお父さんが，その件について君にアドバイスできる最良の人だ。」

(3)「今ちょうど入ってきた少女の名前は何ですか。」

check 2 (1) The man to(about) whom you spoke the other day is my boss. (The man (whom(that)) you spoke to(about) the other day is my boss.)

(2) Mathematics is the subject in which I am interested. (Mathematics is the subject (which(that)) I am interested in.)

解説

〈前置詞＋関係代名詞〉の形にする場合，「that, who は不可」「関係代名詞は省略できない」の２点に注意する。

check 3 (1)あなたに役立つような本だけを読みなさい。

(2)例外のない規則はない。

解説

(1) such 〜 as ...「…するような〜」

(2) but は否定の意味を含む関係代名詞。

1 (1) The woman whom(that) I met at the airport was a Chinese.

(2) The girl who(that) I believed was Mark's girlfriend is Jessica.

(3) This is the restaurant about which I once talked. (This is the restaurant which(that) I once talked about.)

解説

(1)先行詞が人で目的格なので，whom〔that〕を用いる。目的格の関係代名詞は省略可。

(2) I believed *she* was ... の she を，主格の関係代名詞 who〔that〕に変える。

(3) about which もしくは which〔that〕〜 about の形にする。

2 (1) who (2) who (3) whom (4) that (5) which (6) what (7) whose (8) that

解説

(1), (2), (5)は that でも可。

(1)先行詞は「人」で主格。

(2)先行詞は「人」で主格。I think は挿入句。

(3)先行詞は「人」で前置詞 to の目的語なので目的格。to that とはならない。

(4)強調修飾語の the best があるので that。

(5)先行詞は「物」。

(6)先行詞がないことに注意。「この本はまさに私のほしかったものだ。」

(7)所有格。

(8)強調修飾語の the last があるので that。

---

❸ (1) I will show you the computer (which) I bought yesterday.

(2) He is the teacher from <u>whom</u> I borrowed this book yesterday.

(3) Buy it back from the man (<u>whom</u> (<u>that</u>)) you sold it <u>to</u>.

(4) Look at the boy and his dog (<u>that</u> are) running after a fox.

(5) He is not <u>what</u> he used to be.

解説

(1) it と関係代名詞 which が重複している。

(2)「彼は私が昨日この本を借りた先生だ。」

(3) Buy it back from the man you sold it to (him →) whom(省略可).「君がそれを売った人から買い戻しなさい。」

(4)先行詞は「人と動物」なので that。

(5) what he used to be は「昔の彼」という意味の慣用表現。

---

❹ (1) whose, hair (2) that, you

解説

(1) *his* hair is gray と考え,所有格の関係代名詞を用いる。

(2)「あなたはここにとどまりさえすればよい。」→「あなたがすべき唯一のことは,ここにとどまることだ。」先行詞に強調修飾語の the only があるため,関係代名詞は that が適切。

---

17 関係詞 ②   (pp. 36〜37)

check 1 (1) when (2) why (3) where

解説

(1) when = on which

(2) why = for which

(3) where = in which

check 2 (1)モーツァルトは,あなたが彼の音楽をずっと聴いているが,私の大好きな作曲家だ。

(2)私の休暇は,そのときになれば休息をとれるが,間もなくやってくる。

解説

(1) Mozart, you have been listening to *his* music, ... から考える。

(2) My vacation, I can get some rest *then*, ... から考える。

check 3 (1) whichever (2) Whoever

解説

(1)「あなたの好きな本のどれでも持って行きなさい。」

(2)「窓を壊した人はだれでも,弁償しなければならない。」

---

❶ (1) why (2) where (3) where (4) when (5) why

解説

(5)先行詞 the reason を省略している。That's why 〜.「そういうわけで〜」はよく用いられる表現である。

---

❷ (1) that (2) whose (3) where (4) which(that) (5) who (6) where (7) which (8) why

解説

(1)「これがまさに私がずっとさがしている本だ。」

(2)「ジョンは,仕事でたびたび外国へ行く人だ。」

(3)「お話できる静かな場所を見つけましょう。」

(4)「彼のいちばん好きな科目は化学だ。」

(5)「彼女の父は,ガンで死んだのだが,ヘビースモーカーだった。」

(6)「私は本を置き忘れた場所を思い出した。」

(7)「これはシェークスピアが生まれた家だ。」
(8)「彼は十分に運動しない－そういうわけで彼は太りすぎている。」

3 (1) This is how I came to know him
(2) where they were staying for their

解説
(1) *e.g.* This is how the accident happened.「このようにして事故は起きた。」
(2)関係代名詞では the hotel at which they were ... と表現できる。

4 (1) whenever (2) Whoever
(3) wherever (4) whatever

解説
(1)「空腹なときにいつでも食事をする子どもたちがいる。」
(2)「その本がほしい人はだれでも取ってよい。」
(3)「あなたの好きなところどこにでも座りなさい。」
(4)「君が私に頼むことは何でもやってあげよう。」

18 仮定法 (pp. 38〜39)

check 1 (1) were(was) (2) had come
(3) were (4) should

解説
(1)現在の事実に反する仮定…仮定法過去なので動詞・助動詞の過去形を用いる。be 動詞は通例were を用いる。
(2)過去の事実に反する仮定は仮定法過去完了なので過去完了形を用いる。
(3) If S were to 〜, の形は純粋な仮定に用いる。「もし, 私が死ぬことになれば私の家族はどうなるのだろうか。」
(4) If S should 〜, の形は, 実現の可能性の低い仮定に用いる。「万一, 失敗したら君はどうしますか。」

check 2 (1) But (2) Had (3) as

解説
(1) but for 〜 = without 〜「〜がなければ」
(2) If you had come earlier, の If が省略された形で, 倒置の表現。
(3) as if 〜「まるで〜かのように」仮定法の慣用表現。

1 (1) had, could (2) were(was), would
(3) missed, could (4) had, could, have
(5) had, rained, could

解説
(1)現在の事実に反しているので, 仮定法過去。「もし彼に十分なお金があれば, 新車を買えるのに。」
(2)仮定法過去。「もし私が鳥なら, 空を飛ぶだろうに。」
(3)過去の事実に反しているので, 仮定法過去完了。「もし私がそのバスに乗り遅れなかったら, 間に合っただろうに。」
(4)仮定法過去完了。「もし具合が悪くなかったら, 彼らとゴルフができたのに。」
(5)従属節は仮定法過去完了, 主節は仮定法過去にする。「もし昨日, 雨がたくさん降らなかったら, 自転車に乗れたのに。」

2 (1) had, not, been, for
(2) wish, could (3) as, if, were(was)
(4) Had, been (5) time, left

解説
(1) without 〜「〜なしでは」= if it had not been for 〜（仮定法過去完了）, if it were not for 〜（仮定法過去）
(2)「コンサートに行くことができればなあ。」
(3)「私たちの英語の先生はまるで英国人のように英語を話す。」
(4) If I were there, は仮定法過去で現在の事実に反する仮定なので不適。If I had been there, の If を省略し, 倒置する。
(5)慣用表現。〈It is (high) time + S +過去形〉「S がもう〜する時間だ」

3 (1) wish I had read the book before
(2) proposed that she study English every day
(3) had a cold, I could have attended the meeting
(4) it not for your support

解説
(1) I wish のあとに仮定法過去完了が使われている。「試験の前にその本を読んでいればよかったなあ。」
(2)「彼女の先生は彼女に, 毎日英語を勉強するよう提案した。」命令・提案などを表す that 節内では,

主語にかかわらず〈(should +)原形〉を用いる。

(3)「もし，カゼをひいていなかったらその会議に出席できたのに。」

(4)「もし，あなたの助けがなければ，我が社は生き残れないだろう。」Were it ～ は If it were ～ の If を省略して倒置した形。

19 否 定　　　　　(pp. 40〜41)

check 1　(1) No one can solve this problem.
(2) I don't think it will rain tomorrow.
(3) The doctor advised him not to eat too much.
(4) "It's still snowing. Will the plane take off on time?" "I'm afraid not."

解説

(1)英語では，否定語は，できるだけ文頭に置く傾向がある。any ～ not の語順は誤り。not ～ any の語順は正しい。

(2)主節の動詞が，think, believe, suppose の類の場合，that 節ではなく主節を否定することが多い。

(3)不定詞の否定は，原則として not to ～である。

(4) I'm afraid not は，I'm afraid the plane will not take off on time. の下線部を省略したものである。

check 2　(1)①私は君の兄弟の両方とも知っているわけではない。
②私は君の兄弟の両方とも知らない。
(2)①マイクはいつも授業に遅れるとは限らない。
②マイクは決して授業に遅れない。

解説

(1)①部分否定。②全体否定。I know *neither* of your brothers. も②と同じ意味。

(2)①部分否定。②全体否定。

check 3　(1) There is little hope of his success.
(2) Good fortune rarely comes in succession.
(3) She is lonely. She has few friends.
(4) I am so tired that I can hardly walk.

解説

(1)「彼が成功する希望はほとんどない。」
(2)「幸運はめったに続けて訪れない。」
(3)「彼女は孤独だ。ほとんど友達がいない。」
(4)「私はとても疲れているので,ほとんど歩けない。」

1　(1) I can speak neither English nor French. (I can't speak either English or French.)
(2) None of my students work hard.
(3) I don't understand all of these questions.

解説

(1)部分否定→全体否定。「私は英語もフランス語も話すことはできない。」

(2)部分否定→全体否定。「私の生徒はだれ1人として熱心に勉強しない。」

(3)全体否定→部分否定。「私はこれらの問題のすべてを理解しているわけではない。」

2　(1) does, not　(2) free, of(from)
(3) last　(4) not, too　(5) not, before
(6) never(cannot), without

解説

(1) but は否定を含む関係代名詞。
(2) be free of(from) ～「～がない，～を免れている」
(3) the last person to ～「決して～しない人」
(4)「運転するときには，いくら注意してもしすぎることはない。」
(5) It will not be long before ～.「間もなく～する。」
(6)二重否定 never(cannot)... without ～ing「～することなしに決して… しない(できない)」の意味から，肯定になる。「私はこの歌を聞くと，必ず幸せな日々を思い出す。」

3　(1)イ　(2)ウ　(3)イ

解説

(1) cannot help ～ing「～せざるを得ない」
(2) nothing but「～だけ」= only
(3)前出の否定を受けて，〈nor +疑問文の語順〉で「～もまた…でない」の意味。
e.g. A : I don't like dogs.
　　B : Nor do I.

20 接続詞 (pp. 42〜43)

check 1 (1) nor (2) or (3) but (4) and

解説
(1) 否定の内容を受けて，「…もまた〜でない」の意味を表す。　*e.g.* John didn't come, *nor* did his wife.（= and his wife didn't come, either）
(2) 命令文, or 〜.「…せよ，そうでないと〜だ。」
(3) but「しかし」
(4) 命令文, and 〜.「…せよ，そうすれば〜だ。」

check 2 (1) that (2) before
(3) whether〔if〕
(4) though〔although〕

解説
(1) 同格を表す that で，The news = he was still alive の関係になる。
(2) before「〜する前に」
(3) 間接疑問の名詞節を導く whether, if「〜かどうか」
(4) though 〜「〜だけれども」

check 3 (1) but (2) Neither (3) well
(4) but (5) Either

解説
(1) not only A but (also) B「AだけでなくBも」
(2) neither A nor B「A，Bの両方とも〜でない」動詞はBに合わせる。
(3) A as well as B「BだけでなくAも」
(4) not A but B「AでなくB」
(5) either A or B「AかBのどちらか」

1 (1) if (2) Before (3) since (4) As
(5) and (6) or (7) Though (8) that

解説
(1) if「〜かどうか」
(2) before「〜する前に」
(3) 〈It is〔has been〕+ 期間を表す語句 + since 〜.〉「〜以来…だ。」
(4) as「〜するにつれて」「彼は年をとるにつれて，行動的でなくなった。」
(5) 命令文, and 〜.「…せよ，そうすれば〜だ。」
(6) either A or B「AかBのどちらか」動詞はBに合わせる。
(7) though「〜にもかかわらず」
(8) the fact = that 節　同格の that 節。

2 (1) She gave us a CD as well as a book
(2) I've been keeping another seat so that you
(3) Both English and French are spoken in
(4) looks smart as long as she doesn't speak
(5) Unless you have a strong stomach, you had better not drink tap water in

解説
(1) B as well as A (= not only A but (also) B) で「AだけでなくBも」。AとBの語順に注意。
(2) so that + S + can〔will, may〕で「Sが〜するように」。so 〜 that ...「とても〜なので…」と区別すること。
(3)「英語もフランス語も」が主語。
(4) as long as 〜は「〜するかぎり，〜する間は」の意味で，条件・時を表す。程度・限界を表す as far as 〜 という表現もあるため，注意すること。
(5) unless 〜 = if 〜 not「〜でないなら」

3 (1) before (2) that (3) as〔though〕
(4) if〔though〕 (5) because

解説
(1) It will not be long before 〜.「間もなく〜するだろう。」
(2) The trouble is that 〜.「困ったことに〜 だ。」
(3) Young as〔though〕he was, = Though he was young,「彼は若いけれど」
(4) even if〔though〕〜「たとえ〜でも」
(5) not 〜 just because ...「…だからといって〜ない」

21 名詞・冠詞 (pp. 44〜45)

check 1 (1) The police are investigating the murder.
(2) We have collected a lot of information on the matter.
(3) There is not much furniture in his room.

17

解説

(1) the police は複数扱い。

(2) information「情報」は不可算名詞。

(3) furniture は不可算名詞で単数扱い。

check 2 (1) the (2) an (3) The, the

解説

(1) first〔second, third …〕などの序数詞, only, 最上級などには, 定冠詞 the が必要。

(2) hour〔auər〕は母音の発音で始まる語なので, an。

(3)唯一のものには, 定冠詞をつける。

1 (1) work (2) glasses (3) was
(4) baggage (5) a fire (6) are
(7) a bit of advice (8) are

解説

(1)「仕事」の意味の work は不可算名詞。

(2) glass は「ガラス」の意味で不可算名詞,「コップ〔グラス〕」の意味で可算名詞。ここでは「コップ」の意味。

(3) money などの物質名詞は all とともに用いられても単数扱い。

(4) baggage「荷物」は不可算名詞。

(5) fire は「火」の意味で不可算名詞,「火事」の意味で可算名詞。ここでは「火事」の意味。

(6)この場合, 日本人全体を表し, 複数扱い。

(7) advice は不可算名詞。

(8) the + rich = rich people は複数扱い。

2 (1) We usually take a walk after dinner.

(2) I can't do two things at a time.

(3) A stranger caught me by the hand.

(4) How often do you go to the barbar's a month?

(5) He is one of the smartest students in our class.

(6) Would you mind opening the window?

解説

(1) take a walk「散歩する」

(2) at a time「1度に」

(3)体の一部を示す表現。〈前置詞＋ the ＋体の一部〉
  e.g. My teacher hit me *on the head*.

(4) a month「1か月につき」この場合の不定冠詞は

per「〜につき」の意味。

(5)〈the ＋最上級〉

(6)文脈上, window は限定されるので the が必要。

3 (1) cup (2) piece (3) bottle
(4) sheet (5) cake (6) loaf

解説

(1) a cup of 〜「カップ1杯の〜」

(2) a piece of news〔information, advice, furniture, chalk〕

(3) a bottle of 〜「ビン1本の 〜」

(4) a sheet of 〜「1枚の〜」

(5) a cake of 〜「（ケーキのようなかたまり）1個の〜」

(6)「（パンなどのかたまり）1個の〜」

4 (1) ease (2) fun (3) Shakespeares
(4) importance (5) poetry

解説

(1)〈with ＋抽象名詞〉→副詞
  e.g. with care → carefully

(2) fun を be 動詞の補語に用いて,「おもしろいこと」の意味。

(3)固有名詞の普通名詞化。「シェークスピアの作品」

(4)〈of ＋抽象名詞〉→ 形容詞 *e.g.* of use → useful

(5) a piece of poetry ＝ a poem「（具体的な）詩1編」

22 代名詞 ①　　　　　　　　(pp. 46〜47)

check 1 (1) mine (2) yourself (3) It

解説

(1) a friend of mine「私の友達」

(2) help oneself to 〜「自由に〜を食べる」

(3) It costs ... to 〜.「〜するのに…の費用がかかる。」

check 2 (1) not that of a gentleman
(2) those who help themselves

解説

(2) those who 〜「〜する人々」「天は自ら助くる者を助く。」（ことわざ）

1 (1) My sister always looks at herself in the mirror.

(2) The climate of this country is like that of Japan.

(3) My room is not as large as <u>yours</u>.

(4) <u>This album of mine</u> is the only thing to show you.

(5) "Hello. <u>This is</u> Mike Smith speaking."

解説

(1) look at oneself in the mirror「鏡で自分自身を見る」

(2) that は the climate の代わり。

(3) yours ＝ your room と考える。

(4) my などの所有格は，a，an，this，some，no などと並べては用いられない。〈of ＋所有代名詞〉の形で名詞の後ろに置く。*e.g.*（×）this his new car → this new car of his

(5) 電話の慣用表現。This is S peaking.（こちらは S です。）

2 (1) they (2) It (3) himself
(4) themselves (5) we (6) you

解説

(1) 不特定の人々を表す主語は they または people。

(2) that 以下を表す形式主語の It。

(3) for oneself ＝ without help「独力で」

(4) enjoy oneself「楽しむ」

(5) Let's 〜. の構文の付加疑問は Let's 〜，shall we?

(6) 命令文の付加疑問は，〜, will you?

3 (1) yourself, home (2) Those
(3) These

解説

(1) make oneself at home「くつろぐ」

(2) those who 〜「〜する人々」

(3) these days で「近ごろ」。in those days「当時」と混同しないこと。

4 (1) It, that (2) herself (3) it, lot

解説

(1)「彼は正直だと言われている。」It is said that 〜「〜だと言われている。」の形にする。it は形式主語。

(2)「その女性は1人で仕事を終わらせなければならなかった。」by oneself「1人で」

(3)「日本では，6月にたくさんの雨が降る。」天候は，〈we have ＋名詞〉と〈it ＋動詞〉の2通りの表し方がある。

23 代名詞 ②　　　　　　　　(pp. 48〜49)

check 1 (1) Each (2) one
(3) one，the other

解説

(1) every は代名詞としては単独で用いられない。every one，everyone なら正しい。

(2) 不特定の単数可算名詞なので one。

(3) 二者のうち1つを one とすると，他の1つは the other。

1 (1) another (2) the others
(3) others (4) the other (5) another
(6) others (7) the other (8) the others

解説

(1) another「もう1つの〜」

(2) 特定された3つ以上の，one「1つ」と the others「残り全部」

(3) 不特定多数の some「いくつか」と others「残りのうちいくつかの」

(4) 2つのうちで one「1つ」と the other「もう1つ」

(5) another「別のもう1つ」

(6) others「他人」

(7) on the other side of the street「通りの反対側に」

(8) the others「残りのすべての乗客」

2 (1) one (2) either (3) another
(4) others (5) those (6) Both
(7) each (8) any, some (9) another
(10) any

解説

(1) 不特定の単数可算名詞を表す one。

(2) not 〜either「二者のうちどちらも〜でない」

(3) A is one thing; B is another.「A と B は全く別のものである。」

(4) others「他人」

(5) those は the apples を表す代名詞。

(6) play とあるので複数扱いの both が適当。

(7) each は単数扱い，both は複数扱い。on *both sides* of the street なら正しい。

(8) not any 〜「少しも〜がない」，肯定の答えを期待する勧誘・依頼などのときは some を用いる。*e.g.* Will you have some more coffee?（コーヒーをもう少しいかがですか。）

(9) one after another「次々に」の慣用表現。

(10) 条件節 if 〜 の中では any。if (there are) any

(errors)「もし誤りがあるならば」

3 (1) Neither　(2) none
　　(3) the others　(4) others
　　(5) somebody　(6) another
　　(7) Both　(8) Either

解説
(1)「両方とも～でない」の意味で単数扱い。
(2) none「少しも～ない」
(3) 特定された多数のうち, some「そのうちのあるもの」the others「残りの全部」
(4) others「他人」
(5) somebody「すぐれた人」, nobody「取るに足らない人物」
(6)「約束をすることと守ることは別のことである。」
(7)「ケンの両親の両方とも」
(8)「コーヒーと紅茶のどちらがよろしいですか。」「私は気にしません。」

24 形容詞・副詞 (pp. 50～51)

check 1　(1) The noise kept me <u>awake</u> all night.
(2) I want something <u>cold</u> to drink.
(3) He wasted a <u>great</u> deal of money on gambling.

解説
(1) keep ～ awake「～を眠らせない」
(2) something, anything などを修飾する形容詞はその後ろに置く。
(3) a great deal of ～「大量の～」 *cf.* a great number of ～「多数の～」

check 2　(1) late　(2) much

解説
(1) late「遅く」, lately「最近」
(2) 比較級を修飾するのは, much。

1 (1) hardly　(2) a great deal of
　　(3) much　(4) bitter　(5) frightened

解説
(1)「私は, 彼女が英語を話すのが苦手だったとほとんど想像できない。」
(2) money は不可算名詞なので, 数を表す a large

number of は不可。
(3) 形容詞の比較級 more が直後にあるため, much が適切。
(4) Ｓ Ｖ Ｃ の文で, This coffee = bitter の関係。副詞を補語にはできない。
(5) afraid を限定用法で用いることはできない。frightened「おびえた」

2 (1)① 故ジョンソン氏は, 偉大な科学者だった。
　　　② ジョンソン氏は会合に遅れた。
　　(2)① 私は彼の現在の住所を知らない。
　　　② 出席していた人々は全員女性だった。
　　(3)① 彼が明日来るのは確かだ。
　　　② 彼はある理由で明日来ないだろう。

3 (1) Quite <u>a</u> few computers were stolen from the shop
　　(2) My father seldom <u>goes</u> shopping with my mother
　　(3) There <u>is</u> something wrong with this machine

解説
(1) quite a few「かなり多くの」。a があるが複数扱い。
(2) seldom「めったに～ない」のような頻度を表す副詞は, 一般動詞の前, be 動詞のあとに置く。
(3) -thing を形容詞が修飾する場合, 形容詞をあとに置く。

4 (1)ウ　(2)エ　(3)ウ

解説
(1)〈形容詞／副詞 + enough + to 不定詞〉「～するのに十分…」の意味。〈enough + 名詞 + to 不定詞〉の語順との違いに注意。
(2)「運転するときは, 注意してもしすぎることはない。」 *e.g.* I can't thank you too much.「お礼の申しようもありません。」
(3)〈such + 名詞句 + that 節〉「とても～なので…だ」The book was so interesting that …〈so + 形容詞／副詞 + that 節〉と書き換え可。

20

25 前置詞 ①　　(pp. 52〜53)

check 1　(1) at　(2) by　(3) on

解説
(1) arrive at〔in〕〜「〜に到着する」
(2) by 〜「(期限を示し)〜までに」
(3) ある特定の日の午前・午後・夕方は on the morning〔afternoon, evening〕of 〜の形式を用いる。

check 2　(1) At the station I was spoken to by an American.
(2) There were no chairs for us to sit on.
(3) This is the book that I've been looking for.

解説
(1) speak to 〜「〜に話しかける」
(2) sit on 〜「〜に座る」
(3) look for 〜「〜をさがす」

1　(1) between　(2) by　(3) on
(4) above　(5) for, during　(6) within
(7) till　(8) before

解説
(1) between A and B「AとBの間に」
(2) by 〜「(期限を示して)〜までに」
(3) on については, check 1 (3)を参照。
(4) above sea level「海面より上に, 海抜」
(5) for + 期間「〜の間」, during + the や所有格などのついた特定の期間「〜の間」
(6) within 〜「〜以内に」
(7) from 〜 till〔to〕...「〜から…まで」
(8) before 〜「〜の前に」

2　(1) There is something funny about him.
(2) John worked very hard, and before long he became a rich man.
(3) Some people believe in the existence of God.
(4) This writer has been in Japan since 1985.
(5) Don't plant the flowers close to that tree.
(6) The bus will be leaving in twenty-five minutes.
(7) We stopped at a pretty village on the way to London.

解説
(1) about 〜「〜の身辺には」「彼にはどこかおもしろい所がある。」
(2) before long「間もなく」
(3) believe in 〜「〜を信じる」
(4) since 〜「〜以来」
(5) close to 〜「〜の近くに」
(6) in twenty-five minutes「(今から)25分後に」
(7) on the way to 〜「〜に行く途中」

3　(1) He has no friends to play with
(2) The subject my son is interested in is English
(3) We need more money to live on
(4) Can't you concentrate more on (upon) your work

解説
(2) be interested in 〜「〜に興味を持っている」
(3) live on 〜「〜に頼って生活する」
(4) concentrate on〔upon〕〜「〜に集中する」 more は文末でもよい。

26 前置詞 ②　　(pp. 54〜55)

check 1　(1) To　(2) in　(3) over　(4) on
(5) in　(6) to

解説
(1) to one's surprise/regret/joy(感情を表す名詞)「驚いたことに／残念なことに／喜ばしいことに」
(2) be caught in a shower「にわか雨に遭う」
(3) over a cup of tea「お茶を飲みながら」
(4) on 〜「(専門的な内容)に関して」
(5) in spite of 〜「〜にもかかわらず」
(6) thanks to 〜「〜のおかげで」

1　(1) from　(2) of　(3) with　(4) with
(5) by　(6) with　(7) on　(8) of　(9) into
(10) with

解説

(1) suffer from ～「～に苦しむ」

(2) die of〔from〕～「～で死ぬ」

(3) be satisfied with ～「～に満足している」

(4)(5) with は道具，by は交通機関や手段に対して用いる。

(6) have something〔nothing〕to do with ～「～に関係がある〔ない〕」

(7) on duty は「勤務時間中で」，off duty は「勤務時間外で」。so 以下の内容に注意。

(8)〈rob ＋人 ＋ of ～〉＝「(人)から～を奪う」を受動態にした文。

(9) make ～ into ... は「～を…に加工する」。make ～ from ...「…から～を作る」と区別すること。

(10)付帯状況を表す with で，〈with ＋物 ＋形容詞〉「(物)を～したまま」の意味。「口をいっぱいにしたまま〔口に食べ物を入れたまま〕話してはいけない。」

2 (1) Because (2) Thanks (3) way
(4) According (5) instead

解説

(1) because of ～「(理由を示して)～のために」

(2) thanks to ～「～のおかげで」

(3) by way of ～「～経由で」

(4) according to ～「～によると」

(5) instead of ～「～の代わりに」

3 (1)ウ (2)イ (3)ア (4)イ (5)エ (6)イ

解説

(1) angry with ～「～に怒って」

(2)不定詞の意味上の主語を表す。人の性質を表す形容詞の場合，for ではなく of を用いる。

(3)〈(just) in case ＋節〉「～ならば，～だといけないから」

(4)〈over ＋食べ物〔飲み物〕〉「～を食べ〔飲み〕ながら」

(5) far from ～「～から遠い，決して～でない」

(6)〈in ＋色〉「～色の服を着て」